The Australian Women's Weekly Home Library

FRUIT & VEGETABLE COOKBOOK

There are fabulous treats waiting for you in the ever-widening range of fruit and vegetables available these days. New varieties can be explored, so use our recipes to add interest and enjoyment to eating. Most importantly, this book will help you make the most of fruit and vegetables at their peak, when they appear seasonally in large quantities. In the centre of the book is a reference chart which tells when and how to select fresh produce and store it. There is also new information on the 53 fruit and vegetables represented in this book; this was compiled by nutritionist Rosemary Stanton, along with a handy kilojoule/calorie counter.

Pamela Clark
FOOD EDITOR

Assistant food editor:	Barbara Northwood	Production editor:	Maryanne Blacker
Deputy editor:	Enid Morrison	Designer-in-chief:	Brooke Stanford
Chief home economist:	Jan Castorina	Sub-editor:	Mary-Anne Danaher
Home economists:	Jon Allen	Art assistant:	Louise McGeachie
	Jane Ash	Photographers:	Paul Clarke
	Wendy Berecry		Ashley Mackevicius
	Karen Green		Andre Martin
	Sue Hipwell		David Young
	Louise Patniotis	Publisher:	Richard Walsh
	Kathy Wharton	Associate publisher:	Sally Milner
Food stylists:	Jacqui Hing		
	Carolyn Fienberg		
	Rosemary Ingram		
	Jennifer Wells		
Editorial assistant:	Denise Prentice		
Kitchen assistant:	Amy Wong		

Fruit and Vegetable Cookbook.

Includes index.
ISBN 0 949892 87 4.

1. Cookery (Fruit). 2. Cookery (Vegetables).
I. Title: Australian Women's Weekly.

641.6'4

Produced by The Australian Women's Weekly Home Library Division.
Typeset by Photoset Computer Service Pty Ltd, Sydney, Australia
Printed by Dai Nippon Co Ltd, Tokyo, Japan
Published by Australian Consolidated Press, 54 Park Street, Sydney
Distributed by Network Distribution Company, 54 Park Street, Sydney

APPLES

Apples have been gathered as far back as the Stone Age. They were cultivated by the Greeks, ancient Romans and Egyptians. Today there are more than 7000 varieties of apples in the world. Popular varieties in Australia include Granny Smith, Jonathan, Delicious, Sturmer and Gravenstein.

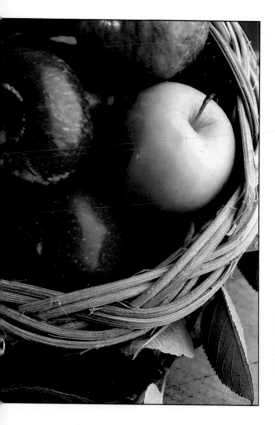

APPLE SOUR CREAM CAKE

Cake can be frozen for a month. Recipe unsuitable to microwave.

250g butter, softened
1 cup castor sugar
4 eggs
1⅓ cups plain flour
¾ cup self-raising flour
300g carton light sour cream
3 medium apples, finely chopped
½ teaspoon ground cinnamon
TOPPING
¼ cup plain flour
¼ cup coconut
¼ cup brown sugar
1 teaspoon ground cinnamon
60g butter
¼ cup flaked almonds

Grease base of 23cm round spring-form tin, line base with greaseproof paper, grease paper. Make topping and refrigerate before preparing cake mixture.

Cream butter and sugar in small bowl with electric mixer, add eggs one at a time, beat until combined. Transfer mixture to large bowl, stir in half the sifted flours with half the sour cream, then stir in remaining flours and sour cream; mix until smooth.

Apple Sour Cream Cake.

High-Rise Apple Pie.

Spread one-third of cake mixture into prepared tin, top with half the apples, sprinkle with half the cinnamon, spread carefully with another third of cake mixture. Top with remaining apple and cinnamon and spread with remaining cake mixture; sprinkle topping evenly over cake.

Bake in moderate oven for about 1¾ hours; cover cake with foil halfway through cooking time to stop topping from over-browning.

Topping: Combine flour, coconut, brown sugar and cinnamon in bowl, rub in butter, press ingredients together; refrigerate until firm. Grate coarsely and add almonds.

HIGH-RISE APPLE PIE

Pie can be frozen for up to 3 months. Recipe unsuitable to microwave.

PASTRY
2½ cups plain flour
⅓ cup icing sugar
185g butter
⅓ cup water, approximately
1 egg white, lightly beaten
1 tablespoon castor sugar
APPLE FILLING
6 large apples, sliced
⅓ cup sugar
½ cup water
CITRUS SAUCE
⅓ cup custard powder

⅓ cup sugar
1½ cups milk
⅓ cup orange juice
2 tablespoons brandy
2 teaspoons grated orange rind
Pastry: Sift flour and icing sugar in bowl, rub in butter. Add enough water to mix to firm dough. Roll out two-thirds of pastry on lightly floured surface till large enough to line base and slightly overlap side of a 20cm spring-form tin. Spoon filling into pastry case.

Roll out remaining pastry, brush edge of pie with egg white, cover with pastry. Press edges of pastry together firmly, trim. Cut a few slits in top of pastry, brush with remaining egg ▶

APPLES

▶ white, sprinkle with castor sugar.

Bake in moderately hot oven 20 minutes, reduce heat to moderate, bake further 30 minutes or until golden brown. Stand 30 minutes before removing from tin. Serve hot or cold with sauce.

Apple Filling: Place apples in saucepan with sugar and water, bring to boil, reduce heat, simmer 10 minutes (or microwave on HIGH for about 5 minutes) or until tender; cool to room temperature.

Citrus Sauce: Combine custard powder and sugar in saucepan, stir in milk and orange juice, stir constantly over heat (or microwave on HIGH for about 3 minutes) until mixture boils and thickens, stir in brandy and rind.

CRUNCHY BAKED APPLES

Recipe unsuitable to freeze.

3 large apples
2 tablespoons lemon juice
1 cup water
2 tablespoons lemon butter
½ cup plain flour
¼ teaspoon ground cinnamon
90g butter
½ cup toasted muesli
½ cup coconut
2 tablespoons brown sugar

Cut apples in half, scoop out core from centre without breaking the skin, brush apples with lemon juice. Place apples, cut side up, in ovenproof dish, add water. Cover, bake in moderate

Crunchy Baked Apples.

oven 30 minutes (or microwave on HIGH for about 6 minutes) or until tender; drain.

Spoon lemon butter into centre of apples. Sift flour and cinnamon in bowl, rub in butter, mix in muesli, coconut and sugar. Lightly press mixture on apples, bake in moderate oven 20 minutes or until topping is golden brown (or microwave on HIGH for about 5 minutes or until heated through).

Serves 6.

APRICOTS

Apricots are a stone fruit from the rose family; they originated in China. They were introduced through the Far East then through the Mediterranean area by the Arabs. To peel apricots, use a vegetable peeler or sharp knife.

FRESH APRICOT JAM

Jam will keep up to 12 months; store in refrigerator. Recipe unsuitable to freeze or microwave.

1kg apricots
½ cup water
¼ cup lemon juice
1kg sugar

Halve apricots and remove stones. Combine apricots, water and lemon juice in large saucepan or boiler; bring to the boil, reduce heat, simmer, covered, for about 15 minutes or until apricots are tender. Add sugar, stir constantly over heat, without boiling, until sugar is dissolved. Bring to the boil and boil, uncovered, without stirring, for about 30 minutes or until jam will jell when tested on a cold saucer. Stir occasionally towards end of cooking to make sure jam is not sticking. Stand 5 minutes before pouring into hot, sterilised jars; seal when cold.

Makes about 5 cups.

CHEWY APRICOT LEATHER

Fruit leather is a chewy, concentrated form of fruit purée, good for snacks or school lunches. This is a useful method of preserving stone fruit when it is cheap or plentiful. Fruit leather will keep up to 6 months or can be frozen for up to 12 months. Recipe unsuitable to microwave.

1kg apricots
2 tablespoons water
Peel apricots and remove stones.

Combine fruit and water in large saucepan, bring to the boil, reduce heat, simmer, covered, until soft and pulpy and as much liquid as possible has been evaporated; time will depend on ripeness of fruit. Stir often to make sure fruit is not burning.

Leave fruit to cool for about 10 minutes, then spread evenly into a foil-lined 25cm x 30cm Swiss roll pan. Dry fruit in a very slow oven, with door slightly ajar, until fruit is dry to touch ▶

ABOVE: Fresh Apricot Jam. LEFT: Chewy Apricot Leather.

APRICOTS

Luscious Apricot Cream.

▶ and without any trace of stickiness. Cool to room temperature, peel away foil. Roll "leather" for easy storage.

Fruit can also be dried in direct sunlight. Cover fruit with a net to protect from insects. If leather takes more than a day to dry, bring it inside at night.

LUSCIOUS APRICOT CREAM

Dessert can be made a day ahead of serving. Recipe unsuitable to freeze or microwave.

1kg apricots
1 cup castor sugar
1 cup water
3 eggs
⅓ cup castor sugar, extra
1 tablespoon gelatine
3 tablespoons lemon juice
¼ cup passionfruit pulp
300ml carton thickened cream

Peel apricots, halve and remove stones. Combine sugar and water in saucepan, stir constantly over heat, without boiling, until sugar is dissolved. Add apricots, bring to the boil, reduce heat, simmer for about 10 minutes, without stirring, until apricots are tender. Remove apricots from syrup, reserve syrup and 8 apricot

halves. Blend or process remaining apricots until smooth.

Beat eggs and extra sugar with electric mixer or rotary beater in top half of double saucepan or heatproof bowl over simmering water until thick, transfer to large bowl; cool.

Sprinkle gelatine over lemon juice, dissolve over hot water, cool to room temperature; do not allow to set.

Stir apricots into egg mixture with gelatine mixture, passionfruit and cream. Pour into a lightly oiled 20cm ring pan, cover, refrigerate overnight. Turn onto serving plate, top with reserved apricots and syrup.

ARTICHOKES

Artichokes (globe) are native to Europe and North Africa. To prepare: cut off stems at base, remove any tough outside leaves and shorten the tips of remaining leaves with scissors.

ARTICHOKES WITH RED WINE DRESSING

This recipe is unsuitable to freeze or microwave.

8 medium globe artichokes
2 hard-boiled eggs, sliced
1 tablespoon chopped fresh chives
RED WINE DRESSING
¼ cup olive oil
¼ cup red wine vinegar
½ teaspoon sugar
½ teaspoon chopped fresh marjoram
½ teaspoon chopped fresh dill
1 clove garlic, crushed

Trim base and outer tough leaves from artichokes. Boil or steam, covered, for about 30 minutes or until tender, drain; cool. Remove any remaining outer leaves that seem tough. Cut hearts in half, place in bowl, add dressing, mix lightly, cover; refrigerate overnight. Serve with egg, sprinkled with chives.
Red Wine Dressing: Combine all the ingredients in jar; shake well.
Serves 4.

▶

BELOW: Artichokes with Red Wine Dressing.

Salad bowl: Incorporated Agencies

ARTICHOKES

ARTICHOKE MUSHROOM CASSEROLE

This recipe is unsuitable to freeze or microwave.

10 medium globe artichokes
30g butter
1 medium onion, sliced
3 bacon rashers, chopped
1 teaspoon caraway seeds, crushed
250g baby mushrooms, halved
2 teaspoons French mustard
¼ cup dry white wine
¼ cup cream
440ml can cream of mushroom soup
2 large potatoes, sliced
paprika

Trim base and outer tough leaves from artichokes. Boil or steam, covered, for about 30 minutes or until tender, drain; cool. Remove any remaining outer leaves that seem tough. Cut hearts in half, place in ovenproof dish.

Melt butter in large frying pan, add onion, bacon and caraway seeds, cook, stirring, until onion is soft. Add mushrooms to pan, cook for 1 minute, stir in 1 teaspoon of the mustard, spread mixture over artichokes.

Heat wine, cream, undiluted soup and remaining mustard in the same pan, pour half over mushroom mixture, top with potatoes then remaining soup mixture. Cover, bake in moderate oven for about 1½ hours or until potatoes are tender. Sprinkle with paprika.

Serves 4 to 6.

ABOVE:
Artichoke
Mushroom
Casserole.
RIGHT:
Stuffed
Artichokes
with
Anchovy
Hollandaise.

Dish: Accoutrement (above). Casserole dish: Made Where (right)

STUFFED ARTICHOKES WITH ANCHOVY HOLLANDAISE

Artichokes can be prepared up to stage of cooking a day ahead. Make sauce just before serving. Recipe unsuitable to freeze or microwave.

6 medium globe artichokes
1 tablespoon oil
2 cloves garlic, crushed
1 medium onion, finely chopped
4 bacon rashers, chopped
3 cups stale breadcrumbs
2 tablespoons chopped fresh basil
2 tablespoons grated parmesan
**   cheese**
1 egg, lightly beaten
½ cup oil, extra
½ cup dry white wine
¼ cup lemon juice
ANCHOVY HOLLANDAISE
4 egg yolks
2 canned anchovy fillets, drained
2 teaspoons French mustard
1 tablespoon lemon juice
125g butter

Cut base from artichokes so they sit flat. Remove outside leaves, shorten

Plate: Villa Italiana

Warm Artichoke Salad with Tarragon Vinaigrette.

tips of remaining leaves with scissors.

Heat oil in frying pan, add garlic, onion and bacon, stir constantly over heat until onion is soft, stir in breadcrumbs and basil, stir over heat further minute. Remove pan from heat, stir in cheese and egg.

Starting from the outside of each artichoke, press stuffing between leaves until artichokes are packed tightly. Place in single layer in baking dish, pour over combined extra oil, wine and lemon juice, bake, uncovered, for about 40 minutes or until artichokes are tender; brush occasionally with oil mixture during cooking. Serve topped with anchovy hollandaise.

Anchovy Hollandaise: Blend or pro-cess egg yolks, anchovy fillets, mustard and lemon juice until smooth. While motor is operating, gradually pour in hot, bubbly butter, process until thick.

Serves 6.

WARM ARTICHOKE SALAD WITH TARRAGON VINAIGRETTE

This recipe is unsuitable to freeze or microwave.

8 medium globe artichokes
45g butter
250g baby mushrooms, sliced
125g salami, chopped
8 green shallots, chopped

TARRAGON VINAIGRETTE
2 tablespoons tarragon vinegar
1 tablespoon olive oil
1 clove garlic, crushed
1 teaspoon seeded mustard

Trim base and outer tough leaves from artichokes. Boil or steam, covered, for about 30 minutes or until tender, drain; cool. Remove any remaining tough outer leaves. Cut hearts into quarters. Heat butter in frying pan, add mushrooms, salami and shallots, stir constantly over heat until mushrooms are soft. Add artichoke hearts and vinaigrette, stir gently until heated through.

Tarragon Vinaigrette: Combine all ingredients in jar, shake well.

Serves 4.

ASPARAGUS

Asparagus originated in eastern Mediterranean lands and Asia Minor. The Romans cultivated asparagus from wild plants around 200BC. To prepare: bend each spear near the cut end, and you will feel a spot where the spear breaks easily; break off this tough end and discard. Peel the tiny nodules gently from thick part of spear, using a vegetable knife or peeler.

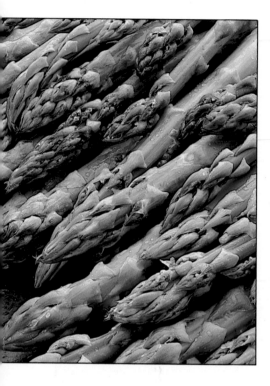

ASPARAGUS ANCHOVY SALAD

Recipe unsuitable to freeze.

250g bunch asparagus
1 small onion, chopped
⅓ cup black olives, chopped
2 hard-boiled egg yolks
ANCHOVY DRESSING
4 anchovy fillets, drained
1 clove garlic
1 tablespoon chopped fresh parsley
2 tablespoons olive oil
3 tablespoons oil
½ cup dry white wine
2 tablespoons lemon juice
½ teaspoon sugar

Boil, steam or microwave asparagus until tender; drain, rinse under cold water, drain. Place asparagus on serving plate, top with onion, olives and dressing; sprinkle with sieved yolks.
Anchovy Dressing: Process or blend all ingredients until smooth.
Serves 2.

PASTA WITH CREAMY ASPARAGUS AND PINE NUTS

Recipe unsuitable to freeze.

2 x 250g bunches asparagus
2 teaspoons cornflour
2 x 300ml cartons thickened cream
1 clove garlic, crushed
1 tablespoon lemon juice

2 bacon rashers, finely chopped
¼ cup pine nuts
375g fettucine (pasta)

Cut asparagus into 2cm lengths, boil, steam or microwave until tender; drain. Blend or process half the asparagus until smooth. Blend cornflour with cream in saucepan, stir constantly over heat (or microwave on HIGH for about 3 minutes) until mixture boils and thickens, add garlic, juice and aspara-

gus purée. Cook bacon in frying pan or microwave oven until crisp. Toast pine nuts on oven tray in moderate oven or in microwave oven.

Gradually add pasta to large saucepan of rapidly boiling water, boil for about 10 minutes, uncovered, or until just tender; drain. Stir pasta quickly but gently into hot sauce with bacon, pine nuts and remaining asparagus.
Serves 4.

ABOVE: Asparagus Anchovy Salad. LEFT: Pasta with Creamy Asparagus and Pine Nuts

Asparagus Pesto Pizza

ASPARAGUS PESTO PIZZA

Pesto can be made up to a week ahead; store, covered, in refrigerator or freeze for up to 3 months. Pizza is unsuitable to freeze or microwave.

250g bunch asparagus
2 rounds Lebanese bread
1 small red pepper, chopped
250g mozzarella cheese, sliced
¼ cup grated parmesan cheese

PESTO
1 tablespoon oil
1 tablespoon pine nuts
1 cup fresh basil leaves
1 clove garlic, chopped
2 tablespoons grated parmesan cheese
1 tablespoon oil, extra

Cut asparagus into 2cm lengths, boil, steam or microwave until tender, drain; rinse under cold water, drain. Spread breads with pesto, top with asparagus, pepper and cheeses. Place pizzas on oven trays, bake in moderate oven for about 20 minutes or until topping is golden brown. Cut each pizza in half.

Pesto: Heat oil in saucepan, add pine nuts, stir constantly over heat until lightly browned. Process or blend undrained pine nuts, basil, garlic, cheese and extra oil until smooth.

Serves 4.

AVOCADOS

Avocados are members of the bay tree family. The first known record of the avocado is in Mayan and Aztec picture writings from 300BC. To remove the stone easily, cut avocado in half, hold the half with stone in one hand and hit the stone with the blade of a heavy knife. Twist the knife and the stone will come out neatly. Once an avocado is cut it will darken, so brush the cut surface with lemon juice.

Smoked Turkey Salad with Avocado Dressing.

AVOCADO SALMON QUICHE

This recipe is unsuitable to freeze or microwave.

PASTRY
2 cups plain flour
125g butter
¼ cup water, approximately
AVOCADO SALMON FILLING
220g can salmon, drained
½ cup grated tasty cheese
4 green shallots, chopped
¾ cup milk
¾ cup cream
3 eggs
2 tablespoons tomato sauce
2 teaspoons canned drained green peppercorns, crushed
1 medium avocado, sliced
Pastry: Sift flour into bowl, rub in butter, add enough water to mix to a firm dough, cover, refrigerate 30 minutes.

Roll pastry large enough to line 23cm flan tin, cover with greaseproof or baking paper, cover paper thickly with dried beans or rice. Bake in moderately hot oven for 7 minutes, remove paper and beans, bake further 7 minutes; cool to room temperature.

Spread salmon mixture into pastry case, pour in egg mixture. Bake in moderate oven 30 minutes or until set.
Avocado Salmon Filling: Break salmon slightly with fork, combine in bowl with cheese and shallots. Combine

milk, cream, eggs, tomato sauce and peppercorns in separate bowl; mix well. Serve the quiche topped with avocado, as shown.

AVOCADO SALAD WITH BLUE CHEESE DRESSING

Recipe unsuitable to freeze.

¼ cup pecans or walnuts, chopped
90g blue cheese
¼ cup olive oil
2 tablespoons lemon juice
1 teaspoon French mustard
¼ cup cream
1 tablespoon chopped fresh chives
2 small avocados, sliced
1 lettuce
Toast nuts on oven tray in moderate oven for about 5 minutes. Process cheese until smooth, gradually add oil, lemon juice, mustard and cream while motor is operating, process until smooth; stir in chives.

Serve avocados with lettuce, topped with dressing and nuts.
Serves 2.

SMOKED TURKEY SALAD WITH AVOCADO DRESSING

Smoked or steamed chicken can be substituted for turkey, if desired. We used a radicchio lettuce, but any lettuce is suitable. Recipe unsuitable to freeze.

500g baby new potatoes
250g smoked turkey, chopped
2 medium avocados, chopped
2 sticks celery, sliced
250g cherry tomatoes
1 lettuce
AVOCADO DRESSING
1 medium avocado
2 tablespoons French dressing
1 tablespoon mayonnaise
⅓ cup light sour cream
Steam, boil or microwave potatoes until tender; cool. Combine turkey with avocados, potatoes, celery and tomatoes, serve on lettuce; top with dressing just before serving.
Avocado Dressing: Blend or process all ingredients until smooth.
Serves 4.

ABOVE:
Avocado
Salmon
Quiche.
LEFT:
Avocado
Salad with
Blue Cheese
Dressing.

BANANAS

Bananas originated in the humid tropical areas of south-east Asia, but the name originated in Africa. Arab traders introduced bananas to Africa and the Mediterranean area.

CRUNCHY BANANA, BACON AND APPLE SALAD

This recipe is unsuitable to freeze or microwave.

6 bacon rashers, coarsely chopped
2 medium apples, chopped
3 medium firm ripe bananas, chopped
1 teaspoon grated lime rind
1 tablespoon lime juice
3 sticks celery, chopped
2 green shallots, chopped
2 tablespoons chopped fresh chives
1 tablespoon chopped fresh parsley
¾ cup mayonnaise
¼ cup plain yoghurt
½ cup chopped pecans or walnuts

Add bacon to frying pan, cook, stirring, until crisp and browned, drain on absorbent paper.

Combine bacon in serving bowl with apples, bananas, lime rind and juice, celery, shallots, chives, parsley, mayonnaise and yoghurt; mix well, serve sprinkled with nuts.

Serves 4 to 6.

WHOLEMEAL BANANA COCONUT CAKE

This recipe is unsuitable to freeze or microwave.

125g butter
1 cup brown sugar, firmly packed
3 eggs
2 medium bananas, finely chopped
⅓ cup coconut
¼ cup wheatgerm
1 cup wholemeal self-raising flour
½ cup white self-raising flour
½ cup milk

Grease 13cm x 21cm loaf pan, line base with greaseproof or baking paper. Cream butter and sugar in small bowl with electric mixer until light and fluffy, add eggs one at a time, beating well after each addition. Mixture may curdle at this stage, but will reconstitute when remaining ingredients are added.

Stir in bananas, coconut and wheatgerm, then half the sifted flours and milk, then remaining flours and milk. Spread mixture into prepared pan and

Crunchy Banana, Bacon and Apple Salad.

China: Polain Interiors

LEFT:
Wholemeal
Banana
Coconut
Cake.
BELOW:
Banana
and Bacon
Chicken
with
Lemon
Sauce.

bake in moderate oven for about 1¼ hours. Stand 5 minutes before turning onto wire rack to cool.

BANANA AND BACON CHICKEN WITH LEMON SAUCE

This recipe is unsuitable to freeze or microwave.

3 bacon rashers, halved
4 chicken breast fillets
2 medium bananas, sliced
plain flour
2 eggs, lightly beaten
1 cup packaged breadcrumbs
30g butter
¼ cup oil
LEMON SAUCE
3 teaspoons cornflour
½ cup water
1 teaspoon grated lemon rind
1 tablespoon lemon juice
2 teaspoons lemon butter
1 small chicken stock cube, crumbled
1 clove garlic, crushed
1 tablespoon sugar

Cook bacon in frying pan until crisp; drain on absorbent paper. Pound chicken with mallet until thin, top each fillet with banana and bacon, fold in half, press edges together firmly. Toss chicken in flour, dip into eggs, toss in breadcrumbs. Heat butter and oil in large frying pan, add chicken in single layer, cook until chicken is tender and golden brown on both sides. Serve with sauce.

Lemon Sauce: Combine blended cornflour and water with remaining ingredients in small saucepan, stir constantly over heat (or microwave on HIGH for 3 minutes) until sauce boils and thickens.

Serves 4.

China: Wedgwood; table: Keyhole Furniture

BEANS

Beans (French): The word "bean" referred to the broad bean, which is still the principal bean of Europe. The French bean was unknown in Europe before Columbus, and originated in the Americas. To prepare: top and tail and remove strings, if necessary.

China: Limoges

BEANS WITH GARLIC AND BACON

Recipe can be frozen for a month.

500g green beans
5 bacon rashers, chopped
2 cloves garlic, crushed
Cut beans into 2cm lengths. Place bacon in large frying pan, cook, stirring, until crisp (or microwave on HIGH for about 3 minutes). Stir in garlic, cook further 1 minute, stirring. Add beans to bacon, cook, stirring, for about 5 minutes or until beans are bright green and crunchy (or microwave on HIGH for about 3 minutes).
Serves 4.

FRESH BEAN SOUP

Recipe unsuitable to freeze.

15g butter
3 bacon rashers, chopped
1 medium onion, chopped
500g green beans
4 cups (1 litre) water
2 small chicken stock cubes, crumbled
½ cup cream
grated fresh parmesan cheese
Melt butter in large saucepan, add bacon and onion, cook 5 minutes (or microwave on HIGH for 3 minutes); stir occasionally. Add beans, cook 1 minute, stirring. Add water and stock cubes, bring to boil, reduce heat, simmer, covered, 15 minutes (or micro-wave on HIGH for 8 minutes).
Blend or process in several batches until smooth. Return soup to pan, stir in cream, reheat without boiling. Serve sprinkled with cheese.
Serves 4.

ABOVE: Beans with Garlic and Bacon.
LEFT: Fresh Bean Soup.

16

BEANS WITH MINTY YOGHURT DRESSING

Recipe can be made up to a day ahead; it is unsuitable to freeze.

500g green beans
1 medium red pepper, sliced
2 cloves garlic, crushed
¼ cup oil
1 tablespoon white vinegar
4 green shallots, chopped
MINTY YOGHURT DRESSING
⅓ cup plain yoghurt
2 tablespoons chopped fresh mint
⅓ cup sour cream
½ teaspoon paprika
½ teaspoon grated lime rind
2 teaspoons lime juice
2 teaspoons honey

Cut beans into 5cm lengths. Boil, steam or microwave beans and pepper until tender, drain; cool. Combine garlic, oil, vinegar and shallots in bowl, add beans and pepper; refrigerate several hours. Serve with dressing.

Minty Yoghurt Dressing: Combine all ingredients in bowl, mix well.

Serves 4.

Beans with Minty Yoghurt Dressing.

China: Limoges; background: Wilson Fabrics

BEETROOT

Beetroot has been cultivated since prehistoric times, and was originally grown for its leaves. The Romans ate only the tops, reserving roots for medicinal purposes. To prepare: the skins slip off easily after the beetroot are boiled, steamed or microwaved.

Pickled Tarragon Beetroot.

PICKLED TARRAGON BEETROOT

Store pickles in airtight jars in a cool, dark place for up to a year. Recipe unsuitable to freeze or microwave.

6 medium beetroot
1½ cups tarragon vinegar
6 cups water
1½ cups tarragon vinegar, extra
1½ cups brown sugar, firmly packed
1½ teaspoons ground cinnamon
1½ tablespoons grated fresh ginger

Peel beetroot, cut into thick strips. Combine beetroot in large saucepan ▶

BEETROOT

Beetroot Pepper Salad.

▶ with vinegar and water. Bring to boil, cover, reduce heat, simmer for 15 minutes. Stir in extra vinegar, sugar, cinnamon and ginger, bring to boil, reduce heat, simmer further 15 minutes or until beetroot is just tender.

Pack beetroot into hot, sterilised jars, pour liquid over beetroot; seal jars when cold.

Makes about 12 cups (3 litres).

BEETROOT PEPPER SALAD

This recipe is unsuitable to freeze or microwave.

4 medium beetroot
3 whole black peppercorns
2 tablespoons brown vinegar
1 medium red pepper
1 medium green pepper
3 green shallots, chopped
TANGY MUSTARD DRESSING
½ cup olive oil
¼ cup cider vinegar
1 tablespoon seeded mustard
1 tablespoon sugar

Combine beetroot, peppercorns and vinegar in saucepan, cover with water, bring to boil, reduce heat, simmer, covered, for about 30 minutes or until tender. Drain, cool, remove skins.

Cut beetroot and peppers into strips, place in serving bowl, add shallots and dressing just before serving.
Tangy Mustard Dressing: Combine all ingredients in jar, shake well.

Serves 4.

BEETROOT AND BACON SOUP

Soup can be made up to 3 days ahead. Recipe unsuitable to freeze.

3 large beetroot
2 litres (8 cups) water
1 ham bone
15g butter
1 large onion, chopped
1 medium potato, chopped
1 medium carrot, chopped
2 medium tomatoes, chopped
¼ small cabbage, chopped
4 bacon rashers, chopped
1 tablespoon lemon juice
½ cup sour cream

Place beetroot in saucepan, cover with water, bring to boil, reduce heat, simmer, covered, for about 30 minutes or until tender, drain; cool. Peel beetroot, slice thinly. Combine the 8 cups water and ham bone in large saucepan, cover, bring to boil, reduce heat, simmer 20 minutes, strain, discard bone.

Combine butter and onion in large saucepan, cook, stirring, until onion is soft. Add ham stock, potato, carrot, tomatoes, cabbage, bacon and lemon juice, bring to boil, reduce heat, simmer, uncovered, for 30 minutes (or microwave on HIGH for 10 minutes).

Blend or process soup in several batches until smooth, strain, serve topped with sour cream.

Serves 6.

Beetroot and Bacon Soup.

BLUEBERRIES

Blueberries are native to North America and were introduced commercially to Australia around 1980.

Blueberry Lime Sorbet.

Blueberry and Passionfruit Jam.

BLUEBERRY AND PASSIONFRUIT JAM

Jam can be stored in the refrigerator for up to a year. Recipe unsuitable to freeze or microwave.

3 x 250g punnets blueberries
3 cups water
¼ cup lemon juice
2½ cups sugar, approximately
2 passionfruit

Combine blueberries and water in large saucepan or boiler, bring to boil, reduce heat, simmer 20 minutes or until blueberries are tender.

Measure mixture, return to pan with lemon juice, add ¾ cup sugar to each 1 cup of mixture (mixture should not be more than 5cm deep at this stage).

Stir constantly over heat, without boiling, until sugar is dissolved. Bring to boil, boil mixture rapidly for about 20 minutes or until a teaspoon of mixture jells when tested on a cold saucer. Stir occasionally towards end of cooking time to prevent sticking, stir in passionfruit pulp. Stand mixture 10 minutes, pour into hot sterilised jars, cool, seal when cold.

Makes about 3 cups.

BLUEBERRY LIME SORBET

Sorbet can be made up to 3 days ahead. For easier serving, remove sorbet from freezer to refrigerator 30 minutes before serving.

2 x 250g punnets blueberries
2 cups water
½ cup castor sugar
2 teaspoons grated lime rind
¼ cup lime juice
2 egg whites

Combine blueberries and water in saucepan, bring to boil, reduce heat, simmer 15 minutes. Add sugar, stir constantly over heat without boiling until sugar is dissolved. Cool mixture, add lime rind and juice.

Blend or process blueberry mixture until smooth, pour mixture into lamington pan, cover, freeze for about 1 hour or until partly set. Beat blueberry mixture and egg whites in small bowl with electric mixer or processor until combined, return to lamington pan, cover, freeze until set.

Serves 4 to 6.

BLUEBERRY CORDIAL

Cordial will keep refrigerated for 2 weeks. Recipe unsuitable to freeze or microwave

1½ cups sugar
2 cups water
250g punnet blueberries
2 teaspoons tartaric acid

Combine sugar and water in saucepan, stir constantly over heat without boiling until sugar is dissolved. Bring to boil, reduce heat, simmer 10 minutes without stirring. Add blueberries, simmer 5 minutes, crush blueberries slightly with wooden spoon to release the colour from the fruit. Blend or process blueberry mixture until smooth, add tartaric acid, strain, discard skins. Cool before bottling; seal when cold.

Makes about 4 cups (1 litre).

Blueberry Cordial.

BROCCOLI

Broccoli belongs to the cabbage family and was cultivated in Italy as far back as the 16th century. The word comes from "brocco", meaning arm or branch. To prepare: cut off heavy woody stems but cook the rest along with the flowerets.

BROCCOLI CHEESE SOUFFLE

This recipe is unsuitable to freeze or microwave.

2 tablespoons packaged breadcrumbs
500g broccoli
60g butter
1 medium onion, chopped
2 tablespoons plain flour
¾ cup milk
3 eggs, separated
¼ cup grated tasty cheese
1 egg white

Grease 4 soufflé dishes (1 cup capacity), sprinkle with breadcrumbs. Boil, steam or microwave broccoli until very tender; drain.

Melt 1 tablespoon of the butter in saucepan, stir in onion, cook until soft, then blend or process with broccoli until smooth.

Melt remaining butter in saucepan, stir in flour, cook for 1 minute, stirring; gradually stir in milk. Stir constantly over heat (or microwave on HIGH for 3 minutes; stir occasionally) until mixture boils and thickens.

Stir in egg yolks and cheese, then broccoli mixture; stir until smooth.

Beat the 4 egg whites in medium bowl until firm peaks form, then fold through broccoli mixture in 2 batches. Pour into dishes, bake in moderately hot oven for 30 minutes, serve soufflés immediately.

Serves 4.

LEMON AND MUSTARD BROCCOLI FLAN

This recipe is unsuitable to freeze or microwave.

PASTRY
1¼ cups plain flour
90g butter
1 egg yolk
1 tablespoon water, approximately
FILLING
500g broccoli
6 green shallots, chopped
3 teaspoons grated lemon rind
1 tablespoon seeded mustard
300ml carton cream
3 eggs, lightly beaten
1 cup grated tasty cheese
Pastry: Sift flour into bowl, rub in

Broccoli Cheese Soufflé.

Dishes: Australian East India Company

Lemon and Mustard Broccoli Flan.

butter, add egg yolk and enough water to make ingredients cling together. Knead gently on lightly floured surface until smooth, cover; refrigerate 30 minutes. Roll pastry large enough to line deep 23cm flan tin, trim edges.

Cover pastry with greaseproof or baking paper, fill with dried beans or rice. Bake in moderately hot oven for 7 minutes, remove paper and beans, bake further 7 minutes or until golden brown; cool.

Spread shallot mixture evenly over pastry, top with broccoli in single layer. Gradually pour egg mixture over broccoli, sprinkle with cheese. Bake in moderate oven for about 40 minutes or until set and golden brown. Allow flan to stand 5 minutes before serving.

Filling: Cut broccoli into small flowerets. Boil, steam or microwave until tender, drain; rinse under cold water, drain. Combine shallots, lemon rind and mustard.

Heat cream in small saucepan until nearly boiling, remove from heat, gradually whisk in eggs.

►

BROCCOLI

▶ BROCCOLI WITH SPICY SEAFOOD COCONUT SAUCE

This recipe is unsuitable to freeze or microwave.

750g broccoli
500g uncooked king prawns
500g squid hoods
2 tablespoons oil
500g fish fillets, chopped
1 medium onion, chopped
1 clove garlic, crushed
1 small fresh red chilli, chopped
2 tablespoons curry powder
340ml can coconut cream
½ cup thickened cream
1 medium red pepper, chopped
1 tablespoon chopped fresh mint
2 teaspoons chopped fresh
  coriander
1 teaspoon sugar

Cut broccoli into flowerets. Shell and devein prawns. Cut squid into rings.

Heat oil in frying pan, gradually add fish to pan in single layer. Cook fish on both sides until golden brown, drain. Add onion, garlic, chilli and curry powder to pan, cook until onion is soft. Stir in coconut cream, cream and broccoli, bring to boil, reduce heat, simmer for 10 minutes. Add pepper, fish, prawns, squid, mint, coriander and sugar. Cover, simmer for about 3 minutes or until prawns are tender.

Serves 6.

Broccoli with Spicy Seafood Coconut Sauce.

Dish: The Bay Tree; tiles: Pazotti

BRUSSELS SPROUTS

Brussels sprouts are descendants of the wild cabbage and were first cultivated in Brussels in the 13th century. To prepare: peel away any tough outer leaves, trim stems neatly, cut a cross in stem end to make cooking a little quicker.

BRUSSELS SPROUTS AND HAM LASAGNE

Lasagne can be made a day ahead. It is unsuitable to freeze or microwave.

750g Brussels sprouts
¼ cup lemon juice
1 tablespoon seeded mustard
4 green shallots, chopped
375g ham, finely chopped
250g packet traditional lasagne
  sheets
2 medium tomatoes, sliced
¼ cup grated parmesan cheese
TASTY CHEESE SAUCE
60g butter
2 tablespoons plain flour
2 cups milk
1½ cups grated tasty cheese
Boil, steam or microwave sprouts until

tender, drain; rinse under cold water. Cut sprouts into quarters, combine in bowl with lemon juice, mustard, shallots and ham.

Add lasagne sheets gradually to large saucepan of boiling water, boil rapidly, uncovered, for about 10 minutes or until just tender; drain.

Place half the lasagne sheets in single layer over base of greased oven-proof dish (2 litre capacity), top with half the cheese sauce and half the sprouts mixture. Top with remaining lasagne sheets, spread with remaining cheese sauce and sprouts mixture. Top with tomatoes, sprinkle with cheese. Bake, covered, in moderate oven for 30 minutes. Remove cover, bake further 15 minutes.

Tasty Cheese Sauce: Melt butter in saucepan, stir in flour, stir constantly over heat for 1 minute, gradually stir in milk. Stir constantly over heat (or microwave on HIGH for about 3 minutes) until sauce boils and thickens. Add cheese, stir until melted.

Serves 4.

BRUSSELS SPROUTS AND BACON STRUDEL

This recipe is unsuitable to freeze or microwave.

1 tablespoon oil
2 cloves garlic, crushed
1½ cups stale breadcrumbs
30g butter
4 bacon rashers, chopped
1 medium onion, chopped
750g Brussels sprouts, chopped
400g can sweet red peppers, drained, chopped
12 sheets fillo pastry
60g butter, melted, extra
CURRY CHEESE SAUCE
30g butter
½ teaspoon curry powder
2 tablespoons plain flour
1 cup milk
1 cup grated tasty cheese

Heat oil in large frying pan, add garlic and crumbs, toss until crumbs are golden brown, drain on absorbent paper. Melt butter in frying pan, add bacon and onion, cook until bacon is browned and onion soft; stir occasionally. Add sprouts, cook until just tender, stir in peppers.

Place one sheet of pastry on bench (cover remaining pastry with grease-proof paper and damp tea-towel), brush with some of the extra butter. Sprinkle with a tablespoon of breadcrumb mixture. Top with another sheet of pastry. Repeat buttering and layering until half the pastry and crumb mixture are used.

Place half the sprouts filling along the long side of pastry, leaving a 5cm border. Fold edges of pastry in, roll up carefully like a Swiss roll. Repeat the ▶

Brussels Sprouts and Ham Lasagne.

Brussels Sprouts and Bacon Strudel.

BRUSSELS SPROUTS

▶ process with all pastry and filling.

Place strudels on oven trays, brush with remaining butter, bake in moderate oven for about 30 minutes. Serve with sauce.

Curry Cheese Sauce: Melt butter in saucepan, stir in curry powder and flour, stir over heat 1 minute. Gradually stir in milk, stir constantly over heat until sauce boils and thickens. Add cheese, stir until melted.

Serves 6.

BRUSSELS SPROUTS WITH BLUE CHEESE SAUCE

Recipe unsuitable to freeze.

1kg Brussels sprouts

30g butter
1 clove garlic, crushed
1 medium onion, chopped
125g blue cheese, crumbled
1 tablespoon cornflour
½ cup cream
½ cup milk
2 teaspoons grated lemon rind
2 tablespoons lemon juice
LEMONY CRUMB TOPPING
30g butter
1 tablespoon oil
1½ cups stale breadcrumbs
¼ cup grated parmesan cheese
2 teaspoons grated lemon rind

Boil, steam or microwave sprouts until just tender, drain.

Heat butter in saucepan, add garlic and onion, cook, stirring, until onion is

Brussels Sprouts with Blue Cheese Sauce.

soft. Add cheese, cook, stirring, until melted. Stir in cornflour blended with cream and milk, cook, stirring (or microwave on HIGH for about 3 minutes), until mixture boils and thickens. Stir in rind and juice.

Place sprouts in greased ovenproof dish, top with sauce, then topping. Bake in moderate oven 15 minutes.

Lemony Crumb Topping: Heat butter and oil in frying pan, add breadcrumbs, cook, stirring, until golden brown, stir in cheese and rind.

Serves 6.

CABBAGES

Cabbage is thought to have originated in Asia Minor and the eastern Mediterranean area. Cabbage was known to have grown wild for centuries near European and English sea coasts. It is uncertain who was responsible for the first cultivation of cabbages.

RED CABBAGE AND RICE SLICE

You will need to cook ⅔ cup rice for this dish. Recipe unsuitable to freeze or microwave.

30g butter
½ medium red cabbage, shredded
1 medium apple, grated
¼ cup sultanas
2 bacon rashers, chopped
3 green shallots, chopped
2 tablespoons chopped pecans or walnuts
2 cups cooked rice
pinch ground cumin
2 eggs
1 cup grated tasty cheese

Grease 23cm square slab pan, line base and sides with greaseproof or baking paper, grease paper.

Melt half the butter in large saucepan, add cabbage, apple and sultanas, cover, cook over low heat for about 20 minutes or until cabbage is tender; stir ▶

Screen: John Normyle

Red Cabbage and Rice Slice.

27

CABBAGES

▶ occasionally. Transfer to bowl.

Melt remaining butter in frying pan, add bacon, shallots and nuts, cook, stirring, until bacon is lightly browned. Stir in rice, cumin and one of the lightly beaten eggs.

Press rice mixture into prepared pan. Add remaining lightly beaten egg to cabbage mixture, spread over rice mixture. Cover with greaseproof or baking paper, then foil.

Place pan in baking dish with enough hot water to come half-way up sides of pan, bake in moderate oven for 20 minutes, remove pan from water and top slice with cheese. Bake further 10 minutes in moderate oven until cheese is melted; stand 10 minutes before cutting.

CABBAGE FRANKFURT PIZZA

This recipe is unsuitable to freeze or microwave.

60g butter
½ medium cabbage, finely shredded
2 cloves garlic, crushed
2 eggs, lightly beaten
½ cup plain flour
2 medium tomatoes, thinly sliced
6 green shallots, chopped
4 thick continental frankfurts, sliced
1½ cups grated tasty cheese

Heat butter in frying pan, add cabbage and garlic, stir over heat until cabbage is just tender, cool to room temperature in pan. Stir in eggs, then flour. Press evenly over base of greased 30cm pizza pan. Bake in moderately hot oven for 10 minutes.

Place tomatoes evenly over cabbage base, sprinkle with shallots, frankfurts, then cheese. Bake in moderate oven for about 30 minutes or until pizza is browned.

CHINESE CABBAGE WITH BARBECUED PORK

Barbecued pork is available in Asian food stores. Recipe is unsuitable to freeze or microwave.

2 tablespoons oil
2 cloves garlic, crushed
1 teaspoon chopped fresh ginger
4 green shallots, chopped
1 medium Chinese cabbage, shredded
1 large onion, coarsely chopped
500g barbecued pork
1 teaspoon cornflour
¼ cup water
1 tablespoon oyster sauce
1 tablespoon hoisin sauce

Heat 1 tablespoon of the oil in wok or frying pan, add half the garlic and ginger and all the shallots, stir-fry for

Cabbage Frankfurt Pizza.

Chinese Cabbage with Barbecued Pork.

30 seconds. Add cabbage, stir-fry for 1 minute; place on serving plate.

Wipe wok clean with absorbent paper. Heat remaining oil in wok, add onion and remaining garlic and ginger,

stir-fry for 1 minute. Add pork, blended cornflour and water and sauces, stir-fry until mixture boils and thickens. Serve over cabbage.

Serves 4.

Plate: Made Where

Plate & terracotta urn: John Normyle; wire basket: The Country Trader

CARROTS

Carrots are biennial herbs of the parsley family; they originally came from Afghanistan and surrounding countries. To prepare: old, large carrots need to be scraped with a knife or peeled with a vegetable peeler. Young carrots do not need peeling.

Basket: Keyhole Furniture

Moist Carrot Ginger Cake.

MOIST CARROT GINGER CAKE

You will need to grate about 2 large carrots for this recipe. Cake will freeze for 3 months. Recipe unsuitable to microwave.

1 cup self-raising flour
1 teaspoon bicarbonate of soda
½ teaspoon ground cinnamon
½ teaspoon ground cloves
1 cup brown sugar, firmly packed
1½ cups finely grated carrot
½ cup sultanas
½ cup finely chopped glacé ginger
½ cup finely chopped walnuts
⅔ cup oil
2 eggs, lightly beaten
CREAM CHEESE FROSTING
60g packaged cream cheese, softened
30g soft butter
1 teaspoon grated lemon rind
1½ cups icing sugar

Grease 14cm x 25cm loaf pan, line base with paper, grease paper.

Sift flour, soda and spices into bowl, stir in sugar, carrot, sultanas, ginger and nuts; stir in combined oil and eggs. Beat on medium speed with electric mixer for 5 minutes. Pour into prepared pan, bake in moderately slow oven for about 1 hour. Stand 5 minutes before turning onto wire rack to cool. When cold, spread with frosting.

Cream Cheese Frosting: Beat cream cheese, butter and lemon rind in small bowl with electric mixer until smooth, gradually beat in sifted icing sugar.

▶

29

LEFT: Carrot Cheese Parcels.
BELOW: Warm Carrot Mousses.

► WARM CARROT MOUSSES

This recipe is unsuitable to freeze or microwave.

45g butter
3 cloves garlic, crushed
7 medium carrots, sliced
1½ cups water
1 small chicken stock cube, crumbled
¼ cup fresh coriander leaves
3 eggs, lightly beaten
TOMATO SAUCE
½ cup tomato purée
¼ cup cream

Heat butter in saucepan, add garlic and carrots, stir until lightly browned. Add water and stock cube, bring to the boil; reduce heat, simmer, covered, until tender. Strain carrots, reserving quarter cup stock. Blend or process carrots, reserved stock and coriander until smooth. Cool mixture slightly, then stir in eggs. Spoon mixture into 6 greased moulds (half cup capacity), place in baking dish with enough hot water to come halfway up sides of moulds. Bake in moderately slow oven for about 40 minutes or until just set.

Turn onto serving plates, serve warm with sauce.

Tomato Sauce: Combine tomato purée and cream in saucepan, cook until heated through.

Serves 6.

CARROT CHEESE PARCELS

You will need to grate about 6 medium carrots for this recipe. Recipe unsuitable to freeze or microwave.

30g butter
1 small onion, finely chopped
4½ cups coarsely grated carrot
250g cottage cheese
2 tablespoons chopped fresh chives
1 egg, beaten
8 sheets fillo pastry
60g butter, melted, extra
½ cup grated parmesan cheese

Melt butter in saucepan, add onion, cook, stirring, until onion is soft. Combine onion, carrot, cottage cheese, chives and egg in bowl, mix well.

Cut fillo sheets in half, place 2 sheets on bench, cover remaining pastry with greaseproof paper, then a damp cloth to prevent drying. Brush 1 sheet of pastry with extra butter, sprinkle with parmesan cheese, top with another sheet of pastry, brush with butter, sprinkle with more cheese.

Place tablespoonfuls of carrot mixture on one end of pastry, fold in sides and roll up like a Swiss roll. Repeat with remaining pastry and carrot mixture. Place on greased oven tray, brush with butter; bake in moderate oven for about 20 minutes or until golden brown.

Makes 8.

CAULIFLOWER

Cauliflower is a member of the cabbage family, and originated in Asia Minor and the Mediterranean area. The word "cauliflower" comes from two Latin terms and literally means "cabbage flower". To prepare: cut away woody stems and leaves, use flowerets and attached stems.

CAULIFLOWER BACON SOUP

Soup can be made a day before required or frozen for 2 months.

½ **large cauliflower**
3 **bacon rashers, chopped**
1 **medium onion, finely chopped**
4 **cups water**
2 **small chicken stock cubes, crumbled**
¼ **cup cream**
2 **tablespoons chopped fresh parsley**

Cut cauliflower into flowerets. Combine bacon and onion in large saucepan, cook, stirring, until onion is soft. Add cauliflower, water and stock cubes, bring to boil, reduce heat, simmer, covered, for about 20 minutes (or microwave on HIGH for about 10 minutes) or until cauliflower is soft.

Blend or process the mixture in batches until smooth. Return the soup to saucepan, bring to the boil, add cream and parsley, reheat soup, stirring constantly, without boiling.

Serves 4.

▶

Saucepan: The Bay Tree

Cauliflower Bacon Soup.

CAULIFLOWER

► CAULIFLOWER AND PEPPER PICKLES

Pickles will keep for a year stored in a cool dark place. Recipe unsuitable to freeze or microwave.

1 medium cauliflower
2 medium onions
1 medium red pepper
1 tablespoon coarse cooking salt
1 cup white vinegar
½ cup sugar
½ teaspoon ground allspice (pimento)
2 whole cloves
1 bay leaf
1 tablespoon curry powder
1 tablespoon dry mustard
1 tablespoon seeded mustard
1 teaspoon turmeric
1 tablespoon plain flour
¼ cup white vinegar, extra

Cut cauliflower into small flowerets, chop onions and pepper into similar sized pieces. Place all vegetables in large bowl, sprinkle with salt, mix well, cover, stand overnight.

Next day, rinse well under cold water; drain well. Combine vinegar, sugar, allspice, cloves and bay leaf in large saucepan, bring to the boil, add vegetables, cover, simmer for about 20 minutes or until vegetables are just tender; stir occasionally.

Blend remaining ingredients in bowl with extra vinegar, stir into vegetable mixture, stir constantly over heat until mixture boils and thickens. Pour into hot sterilised jars; seal when cold.

Makes about 4 cups.

ABOVE: *Cauliflower and Pepper Pickles.* BELOW: *Cauliflower and Salami in Tomato Sauce.*

CAULIFLOWER AND SALAMI IN TOMATO SAUCE

Recipe can be made a day ahead; it is unsuitable to freeze or microwave.

½ medium cauliflower
2 tablespoons olive oil
2 cloves garlic, crushed
1 medium onion, coarsely chopped
2 tablespoons tomato paste
125g salami, chopped
425g can tomatoes
½ teaspoon dried oregano leaves
400g can sweet red peppers, drained, chopped
½ teaspoon sugar
1 teaspoon drained canned green peppercorns, crushed
1 tablespoon chopped fresh basil

Cut cauliflower into flowerets. Heat oil in large saucepan, add garlic and onion, cook, stirring, until onion is soft. Stir in cauliflower, tomato paste, salami, undrained crushed tomatoes, oregano, peppers, sugar and peppercorns. Bring to boil, reduce heat, simmer, covered, for about 20 minutes or until cauliflower is tender. Stir in basil.

Serves 4.

CELERY

Celery is a member of the carrot family and has been known for thousands of years. The ancient Greeks and Romans used it for medicinal purposes. It was cultivated in Italy and France around the 16th century.

CREAM OF CELERY AND ORANGE SOUP

Soup can be frozen for 2 months.

60g butter
1 clove garlic, crushed
1 medium onion, chopped
1 medium bunch celery, chopped
2 small chicken stock cubes, crumbled
2½ cups water
1 teaspoon grated orange rind
1 bay leaf
2 medium potatoes, chopped
½ cup sour cream

Heat butter in large saucepan. Add garlic, onion and celery, cook, stirring, until onion is soft. Stir in stock cubes, water, rind, bay leaf and potatoes. Bring to the boil, reduce heat, simmer, uncovered, for about 30 minutes (or microwave on HIGH for about 10 minutes) or until potatoes are tender; discard bay leaf. Blend or process mixture until smooth; strain, return to pan. Add cream, reheat without boiling.

Serves 4.

CREAMY BRAISED CELERY

Recipe unsuitable to freeze.

8 sticks celery
2 bacon rashers, chopped
4 green shallots, chopped
15g butter
⅓ cup sour cream
1½ cups milk
2 tablespoons grated parmesan cheese
2 teaspoons seeded mustard
3 teaspoons cornflour
½ cup water

Cut celery into 5cm strips. Cook bacon and shallots in frying pan; stir constantly until bacon is crisp (or microwave on HIGH for 3 minutes), drain on absorbent paper.

Heat butter in frying pan, add celery, stir constantly over heat for 2 minutes (or microwave on HIGH for 2 minutes). Add sour cream, milk, cheese and mustard, then blended cornflour and water. Stir constantly over heat until mixture boils and thickens, reduce heat, simmer 5 minutes (or microwave ▶

China: Dansab; fabric: Wilson

Cream of Celery and Orange Soup.

▶ on HIGH for 3 minutes) or until celery is just tender; stir occasionally. Serve sprinkled with bacon and shallots.

    Serves 4.

CELERY AND RED PEPPER SALAD

This recipe is unsuitable to freeze or microwave.

3 sticks celery
1 medium red pepper
15g butter
1 medium onion, finely chopped
2 tablespoons pine nuts
MINT AND ORANGE DRESSING
1 teaspoon grated orange rind
¼ cup orange juice
1 tablespoon oil
1 tablespoon chopped fresh mint
½ teaspoon sugar

Cut celery and pepper into 5cm strips. Heat butter in frying pan, add onion, stir constantly over heat until onion is soft; add celery, pepper and pine nuts, stir over heat further minute.

    Transfer celery mixture to large bowl. Add dressing, toss well. Refrigerate salad 30 minutes before serving.

Mint and Orange Dressing: Combine all ingredients in jar; shake well.

    Serves 2.

ABOVE: Celery and Red Pepper Salad. RIGHT: Creamy Braised Celery.

China: Limoges

CHERRIES

Cherries are closely related to the plum and originated in China and North America. To remove seeds: there are several varieties of easy-to-use cherry pitters available from hardware and kitchen stores.

Platter: Incorporated Agencies; sauce boat: Hale Imports

Deluxe Chicken Roll with Cherry Sauce.

DELUXE CHICKEN ROLL WITH CHERRY SAUCE

Recipe can be made up to 2 days ahead; it is unsuitable to freeze or microwave.

No. 15 chicken
60g butter
1 medium onion, chopped
1 clove garlic, crushed
2 tablespoons tomato paste
1 teaspoon chopped fresh thyme
250g chicken mince
250g pork and veal mince
1 tablespoon canned green peppercorns, drained
¼ cup shelled pistachio nuts
1 egg, lightly beaten
1 cup stale breadcrumbs
12 large cherries, pitted
CHERRY SAUCE
1kg cherries, pitted
¾ cup orange juice
¼ cup lemon juice
1½ tablespoons sugar
½ cup water
1 bay leaf
1 green shallot, crushed
1 tablespoon cornflour
2 tablespoons water

Using a sharp knife, remove bones from chicken as follows. Cut off wing tips at the second joint. Cut through skin down centre back. Separate flesh from backbone on one side with tip of knife or scalpel, then, following the shape of the bones, gradually ease flesh carefully away from bones. Repeat with other side of chicken.

Holding rib cage away from chicken, cut breastbone away from flesh. Hold up thigh with one hand, cut around the top of bone to remove flesh, scrape down the bone to next joint, cut around flesh again, scrape down to the end. Repeat with other leg bone and both wings. Turn flesh of legs and wings inside chicken.

Heat butter in frying pan. Add onion and garlic, cook, stirring, until onion is soft. Combine onion mixture in large bowl with tomato paste, thyme, chicken mince, pork and veal mince, peppercorns, nuts, egg and breadcrumbs.

Spoon half the chicken mixture down centre of chicken, place cherries down centre, then spread evenly with remaining mixture.

Fold one side of chicken over chicken mixture, then other side. Sew flesh together, using a needle and dark thread. Tie with string at 3cm intervals to retain shape when cooking.

Place chicken in baking dish, rub with a little oil. Bake in moderate oven for about 1¼ hours or until chicken is tender. Stand 15 minutes, remove string and thread. Serve chicken hot or cold with sauce.

Cherry Sauce: Combine cherries with orange and lemon juice, sugar, water, bay leaf and shallot in large saucepan. Bring to boil, reduce heat, simmer, uncovered, for 10 minutes. Remove from heat, discard bay leaf and shallot. Stir in blended cornflour and water, stir constantly over heat until sauce boils and thickens.

Serves 6.

CHERRIES

ABOVE: Jellied Cherries Jubilee.
RIGHT: Cherries in Brandy.

▶ **JELLIED CHERRIES JUBILEE**

Recipe unsuitable to freeze.

750g cherries, pitted
3 cups water
1 cup sugar
2 cinnamon sticks
2 tablespoons cherry brandy
1½ tablespoons gelatine
¼ cup water

Combine cherries in saucepan with water, sugar and cinnamon sticks. Stir constantly over heat without boiling until sugar is dissolved, bring to boil, reduce heat, cover, simmer for about 15 minutes or until cherries are tender (or microwave on HIGH for about 10 minutes), stir occasionally. Remove cinnamon sticks, cool to room temperature; stir in cherry brandy.

Sprinkle gelatine over water, dissolve over hot water (or microwave on HIGH for 30 seconds), cool, do not allow to set, stir into cherry mixture. Refrigerate until mixture is the consistency of unbeaten egg white; stir occasionally to distribute cherries evenly.

Spoon into lightly oiled 20cm baba or ring pan, refrigerate until set. Turn onto serving plate, serve with cream.

CHERRIES IN BRANDY

Cherries will last indefinitely. Do not allow metal lids to touch the liquid; plastic is best to use. This recipe is unsuitable to freeze or microwave.

1kg cherries, pitted
1½ cups sugar
750ml brandy, approximately

Combine cherries and sugar in sterilised jars with screw top lids. Pour enough brandy over cherries to completely cover them, replace lids.

Stand in a cool dark place for at least 6 weeks before using. Invert jars occasionally to help dissolve sugar. Serve cherries with cream or ice-cream.

CHOKOES

Chokoes originated in South America where they are known as chayotes; another name is christophenes. To prepare: peel large chokoes under cold running water, remove cores from centres. Tiny chokoes up to 5cm long don't need peeling before cooking.

ABOVE: Chokoes with Sour Cream and Bacon.
BELOW: Baked Chokoes with Tomatoes and Onion.

CHOKOES WITH SOUR CREAM AND BACON

Recipe unsuitable to freeze.

2 bacon rashers, chopped
3 medium chokoes, sliced
½ cup light sour cream
¼ teaspoon dried basil leaves
¼ teaspoon dried oregano leaves
½ cup grated tasty cheese
6 green shallots, chopped

Cook bacon in pan (or microwave) until crisp, drain on absorbent paper. Add chokoes to pan with bacon fat, cover, cook gently, turning often, for about 30 minutes (or microwave for about 10 minutes) until chokoes are tender.

Top with combined sour cream, basil, oregano, cheese and shallots, heat gently for a few minutes (or microwave on HIGH for about 1 minute) until cheese is melted. Sprinkle with bacon before serving.

Serves 4.

BAKED CHOKOES WITH TOMATOES AND ONION

Recipe unsuitable to freeze.

4 medium chokoes, chopped
2 medium tomatoes, peeled, chopped
1 medium onion, chopped
1 clove garlic, crushed
30g butter, chopped
2 tablespoons dry white wine
½ teaspoon dried oregano leaves

Place chokoes in ovenproof dish, mix in tomatoes, onion, garlic, butter, wine ▶

CHOKOES

▶ and oregano. Bake in moderate oven for about 45 minutes (or microwave on HIGH for 15 minutes) or until chokoes are tender; stir occasionally.

Serves 4.

GINGERED PEAR AND CHOKO CRUMBLE

Chokoes will take on the flavour of the pears as they cook. Young chokoes will give the best results. Recipe unsuitable to freeze.

2 small chokoes, coarsely chopped
2 medium pears, coarsely chopped
1 tablespoon chopped glacé ginger
2 tablespoons brown sugar
1 teaspoon grated lemon rind
1 tablespoon lemon juice
1 egg, lightly beaten
½ cup thickened cream
NUTTY COCONUT TOPPING
¼ cup brown sugar
¼ cup wholemeal plain flour
¼ cup rolled oats
¼ cup coconut
½ cup chopped pecans or walnuts
60g butter

Boil, steam or microwave chokoes until tender; drain. Combine chokoes in shallow ovenproof dish with pears and ginger. Combine sugar, lemon rind and juice, egg and cream in bowl, pour over choko mixture. Sprinkle with topping, bake in moderate oven 30 minutes (or microwave on HIGH for about 10 minutes) or until topping becomes crisp.

Nutty Coconut Topping: Combine dry ingredients in bowl, rub in butter.

Serves 4.

Gingered Pear and Choko Crumble.

CORN

Corn is native to the Americas and was cultivated for thousands of years before the Pilgrims arrived. Sweet corn is a mutation of the Indian field corn. To prepare: remove silk and outer leaves.

CORN RELISH

Relish will keep in refrigerator for up to a month. This recipe is unsuitable to freeze.

4 medium cobs fresh corn
2¼ cups white vinegar
¾ cup sugar
1 medium onion, chopped
1 small green pepper, chopped
1 small red pepper, chopped
2 tablespoons cornflour
1 tablespoon dry mustard
1 tablespoon seeded mustard
¼ cup white vinegar, extra

Cut kernels from corn cobs, using sharp knife. Combine vinegar and sugar in large saucepan, stir constantly over heat without boiling until sugar is dissolved. Bring to the boil, add corn, onion and peppers, cover, reduce heat, simmer 20 minutes (or microwave on HIGH for 8 minutes). Blend

ABOVE: *Corn Relish.*
LEFT: *Corn and Pepper Fritters.*

cornflour with mustards and extra vinegar, stir into corn mixture, stir constantly over heat (or microwave on HIGH for 3 minutes) or until mixture boils and thickens. Pour relish into hot sterilised jars, seal when cold.

Makes about 2 cups.

MUSTARD CORN WITH BACON

This recipe is unsuitable to freeze or microwave.

30g butter, softened
2 teaspoons brown sugar
2 teaspoons seeded mustard
6 bacon rashers
6 medium cobs fresh corn

Mix butter, sugar and mustard together in small bowl, spread mixture evenly over bacon rashers. Wrap each rasher around a corn cob. Place each cob in a piece of foil; wrap to completely enclose. Place corn in single layer on oven tray, bake in moderately hot oven for about 45 minutes or until corn is tender.

Serves 6.

CORN AND PEPPER FRITTERS

Recipe unsuitable to freeze.

2 medium cobs fresh corn
¼ cup milk
2 eggs, separated
¼ cup polenta (corn meal)
¼ cup self-raising flour
1 teaspoon chopped fresh thyme
1 small red pepper, finely chopped
1 tablespoon oil

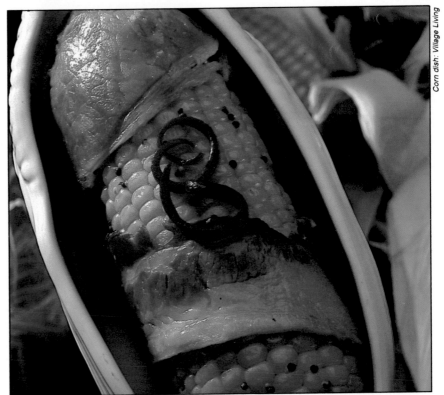

Corn dish: Village Living

Mustard Corn with Bacon.

Boil, steam or microwave corn until tender. Cut kernels from corn cobs, using sharp knife. Blend or process kernels, milk and egg yolks until corn is finely chopped. Combine corn mixture in large bowl with polenta, flour, thyme and pepper. Beat egg whites in small bowl until soft peaks form, fold into corn mixture.

Heat oil in large frying pan, drop tablespoonfuls of mixture into pan. Cook for about 1 minute on each side or until golden brown.

Makes about 20.

CUCUMBERS

Cucumbers are members of the gourd family, and are among the most ancient vegetables. First recordings are in the Himalayas and the northern part of the Bay of Bengal. To prepare: they can be eaten with or without peel; a vegetable peeler removes the peel easily.

APPLE CUCUMBERS WITH BROWN RICE

Recipe unsuitable to freeze.

4 medium apple cucumbers
coarse cooking salt
15g butter
1 small onion, chopped
1 cup brown rice
1 cup water
1 small chicken stock cube, crumbled
1 cup dry white wine
tiny pinch saffron powder
2 bacon rashers, chopped
1 egg, lightly beaten
1 tablespoon chopped fresh chives
¾ cup grated tasty cheese
CHEESY SAUCE
15g butter
1 tablespoon plain flour
1½ cups milk
¼ cup grated tasty cheese
2 tablespoons chopped fresh chives
tiny pinch saffron powder

Peel, halve and remove seeds from cucumbers, sprinkle with salt, stand 15 minutes. Rinse cucumbers under water, pat dry.

Heat butter in frying pan, add onion, cook, stirring, until onion is soft. Add rice, cook, stirring, until rice is opaque, add combined water and stock cube, wine and saffron. Bring to boil, cover, reduce heat, simmer 30 minutes or until liquid is absorbed and rice is tender.

Cook bacon in frying pan (or microwave) until crisp, drain on absorbent paper, add bacon to rice mixture with egg, chives and cheese, mix well.

Place cucumbers, cut side up, in greased, shallow ovenproof dish. Divide filling over cucumbers, bake in moderate oven for 30 minutes (or microwave, covered, on HIGH for about 10 minutes). Serve cucumbers with sauce.

Cheesy Sauce: Heat butter in saucepan, add flour, cook 1 minute, stirring. Gradually stir in milk, stir constantly over heat (or microwave on HIGH for about 3 minutes) or until sauce boils and thickens. Add cheese, chives and saffron, stir until cheese is melted.

Serves 4.

PICKLED CUCUMBERS

We used Lebanese cucumbers in this recipe; however, pickling cucumbers would also be ideal. Recipe unsuitable to freeze or microwave.

2kg green cucumbers
coarse cooking salt
6 cups (1½ litres) white vinegar
1 cup sugar
3 small fresh red chillies
2 tablespoons yellow mustard seeds
2 tablespoons black mustard seeds
1 tablespoon black peppercorns
1 tablespoon dill seeds
6 whole cloves

Cut cucumbers in half lengthways, then into 6cm strips. Place in bowl, sprinkle with salt, stand overnight.

Next day, rinse cucumbers under cold water, drain. Combine vinegar, sugar, chillies, mustard seeds, peppercorns, dill seeds and cloves in large saucepan, bring to the boil, reduce heat, simmer, uncovered, 5 minutes. Add cucumbers, bring to boil, remove from heat immediately.

Using tongs, pack cucumbers into hot sterilised jars, fill with vinegar mixture, seal when cold.

Apple Cucumbers with Brown Rice.

ABOVE: *Pickled Cucumbers.*
RIGHT: *Cucumber Wafer Salad with Peanut Dressing.*

CUCUMBER WAFER SALAD WITH PEANUT DRESSING

This recipe is unsuitable to freeze or microwave.

1 large green cucumber
1 large carrot
250g broccoli
CREAMY PEANUT DRESSING
1 tablespoon peanut butter
¼ cup cream
¼ cup mayonnaise
2 green shallots, chopped

Remove ends from cucumber, cut cucumber lengthways in quarters. Discard seeds, cut each quarter into 5cm lengths. Using a vegetable peeler, peel strips carefully lengthways from each piece.

Cut carrot into 5cm lengths, peel strips from each piece, place into cold water until curled, drain well.

Cut broccoli into flowerets, boil, steam or microwave until just tender, drain; rinse under cold water, drain. Combine vegetables with dressing in serving bowl.

Creamy Peanut Dressing: Combine all ingredients in bowl, mix well.

Serves 4.

CUMQUATS

Cumquats are native to China, Japan and Malaya, but are not a true citrus fruit. They can be eaten whole when young and tender.

Cumquats in Brandy.

CUMQUATS IN BRANDY

For maximum flavour eat cumquats after 3 months, the flavoured brandy is also delicious to drink. This recipe is unsuitable to freeze.

1kg cumquats
2 cups sugar
750ml brandy, approximately

Prick cumquats well with fine skewer. Layer cumquats and sugar in glass jars, pour in enough brandy to cover fruit; seal jars tightly. Store in a cool dark place; turn jars upside down once a week until sugar is dissolved.

CUMQUAT GINGER MARMALADE

This recipe is unsuitable to freeze or microwave.

1kg cumquats
7 cups (1¾ litres) water
7 cups (1¾kg) sugar
1 tablespoon grated fresh ginger

Slice cumquats thinly. Collect seeds, place in small bowl with 1 cup of the water, stand overnight. Combine cumquats in large bowl with remaining water, cover, stand overnight.

Next day, strain seeds, reserve liquid (this now contains pectin, which contributes to the setting of the jam); discard seeds.

Place cumquat mixture into large saucepan or boiler with reserved liquid. Bring to the boil, reduce heat, simmer, covered, for 30 minutes or until cumquats are tender.

Add sugar, stir constantly over heat, without boiling, until sugar is dissolved (mixture should not be more than 5cm deep). Bring to the boil, boil rapidly for about 15 minutes without stirring or until a teaspoon of mixture will jell when tested on a cold saucer; remove pan from heat while testing.

Stir in ginger, stand 10 minutes before pouring into hot, sterilised jars; seal when cold.

Makes about 7 cups.

CUMQUAT SAUCE

This sauce is ideal to serve with cold cuts of meat and poultry; it will keep in the refrigerator for about a month. Recipe is unsuitable to freeze or microwave.

500g cumquats, chopped
2½ cups water
1 tablespoon whole black
 peppercorns
2 bay leaves
1 medium onion, chopped
2 tablespoons cranberry sauce

China: Wedgwood

ABOVE: Cumquat Sauce.
RIGHT: Cumquat Ginger Marmalade.

**2 small chicken stock cubes,
    crumbled**
¼ cup cider vinegar
1 clove garlic, crushed
¼ cup sugar
1 tablespoon brandy

Combine cumquats, water, pepper-corns, bay leaves, onion, sauce, stock cubes, vinegar, garlic and sugar in large saucepan. Bring to the boil, boil rapidly, uncovered, for 10 minutes; reduce heat, simmer, uncovered, for about 15 minutes or until mixture begins to thicken. Discard bay leaves.

Blend or process cumquat mixture until almost smooth; strain. Place mixture in clean saucepan, bring to the boil, reduce heat, simmer, uncovered, for about 10 minutes or until sauce thickens slightly. Stir in brandy.

Makes about 4 cups.

China: Wedgwood; marmalade pot: Reflections Gift Boutique

CUSTARD APPLES

Custard apples are also known as cherimoya in other countries. They are native to tropical America and the Andes in Peru and Ecuador. Only the fleshy pulp is eaten or used in cookery; the skin and seeds are discarded.

CUSTARD APPLE BAVAROIS WITH MANGO

You need 2 cups custard apple purée for this recipe. Bavarois can be made a day before required. Recipe unsuitable to freeze.

3 egg yolks
½ cup castor sugar
1½ cups milk
thin strip lemon rind
1 tablespoon gelatine
3 tablespoons water
2 medium custard apples
300ml carton thickened cream
1 large mango

Beat egg yolks and sugar in small bowl with electric mixer until thick and pale in colour. Gently heat milk with lemon rind in saucepan for about 10 minutes; do not boil. (This is to extract flavour from rind.) Remove rind, whisk egg

Custard Apple Bavarois with Mango.

yolk mixture into milk, stir constantly with wooden spoon over low heat without boiling until mixture thickens slightly, remove from heat; cool to room temperature.

Sprinkle gelatine over water, dissolve over hot water (or microwave on HIGH for 20 seconds), cool to room temperature; do not allow to set. Stir gelatine mixture into custard mixture, pour into large bowl. Stir in strained, puréed custard apples, fold in whipped cream. Pour into 6 lightly oiled dishes (three-quarter cup capacity). Refrigerate several hours or overnight. Turn onto serving plates.

Blend or process mango until smooth, strain, serve with bavarois.

Serves 6.

CUSTARD APPLE ICE-CREAM

You need 2 cups custard apple purée for this recipe. Slice can be frozen several days ahead of serving.

1 teaspoon gelatine
3 teaspoons water
3 egg yolks
⅓ cup castor sugar
½ cup milk
1 teaspoon vanilla essence
2 medium custard apples
300ml carton thickened cream

Line 19cm x 29cm lamington pan with foil. Add gelatine to water, dissolve over hot water (or microwave on HIGH for 15 seconds). Combine egg yolks and sugar in bowl, whisk or beat over simmering water until thick and creamy. Add milk and essence, stir constantly over water until mixture is slightly thickened.

Stir in gelatine mixture, pour into large bowl, cool; do not allow to set. Stir in strained, puréed custard apples and whipped cream. Pour into pan, cover with foil, freeze overnight.

CUSTARD APPLE EGG NOG

2 medium custard apples
2 cups milk
3 egg yolks
2 tablespoons honey

Blend or process custard apples until smooth; strain. Heat milk in saucepan, bring to boil, remove from heat, whisk in egg yolks and honey, stir constantly over low heat, without boiling, until mixture is slightly thickened. Stir in custard apple.

Makes about 4 cups.

ABOVE: Custard Apple Ice-Cream. BELOW: Custard Apple Egg Nog.

Plate: Kosta Boda

Glass mug: KWL Imports

EGGPLANT

The eggplant (aubergine) originated in south east Asia, and belongs to the nightshade family, along with tomatoes and potatoes. Perhaps because of this family tie, the eggplant was called "mad apple" when it was first introduced into northern Europe; botanists of the region believed that eating the vegetable caused insanity. To prepare: use with or without skin; salt removes the bitterness.

CHEESY BAKED EGGPLANTS

You will need to cook ¼ cup rice for this recipe. Recipe unsuitable to freeze or microwave.

**2 medium eggplants
coarse cooking salt
1 tablespoon oil
1 small onion, finely chopped
1 clove garlic, crushed
2 bacon rashers, chopped
2 medium tomatoes, peeled,
    chopped
¾ cup cooked brown rice
1 tablespoon chopped fresh chives
½ cup grated tasty cheese
2 tablespoons grated parmesan
    cheese**

Slice eggplants in half lengthways, scoop out flesh, leaving 2cm shell; sprinkle inside shells and scooped flesh with salt; stand 30 minutes. Rinse under water to remove salt; drain on absorbent paper.

Chop flesh roughly. Heat oil in saucepan, add onion, garlic and bacon, cook, stirring, for about 5 minutes or until soft. Add tomatoes and flesh, cover, cook over heat for about 2 minutes or until soft.

Add ¼ cup of the rice, mix well, spoon into eggplant. Combine remaining rice, chives and cheeses in small bowl, sprinkle evenly over eggplant. Place on lightly greased oven tray, bake in moderate oven for about 20 minutes or until hot.

Serves 4.

MOUSSAKA

Moussaka is best cooked the day before required for easier cutting. Recipe unsuitable to freeze.

**1 large eggplant, thinly sliced
coarse cooking salt
oil
2 medium potatoes, thinly sliced
2 tablespoons packaged
    breadcrumbs
3 tablespoons grated parmesan
    cheese**
MEAT LAYER
**1 tablespoon oil
1 medium onion, chopped
1 clove garlic, crushed**

Cheesy Baked Eggplants.

Dish & spoon: The Bay Tree; tiles: Pazotti

Moussaka.

1kg minced lamb
¼ cup chopped fresh parsley
425g can tomatoes
2 tablespoons tomato paste
½ cup dry red wine
½ teaspoon dried oregano leaves
¼ teaspoon ground cinnamon
CHEESE SAUCE LAYER
60g butter
⅓ cup plain flour
1¾ cups milk
½ cup cream
¼ teaspoon ground nutmeg
⅓ cup grated parmesan cheese
1 egg, lightly beaten

Sprinkle eggplant with salt; stand 30 minutes, rinse under cold water and pat dry with absorbent paper.

Heat oil in large frying pan, cook potatoes and eggplant in batches until tender, drain on absorbent paper.

Lightly grease ovenproof dish (8 cup (2 litre) capacity), sprinkle base with half the breadcrumbs. Layer half the eggplant in dish, sprinkle with a third of parmesan cheese and spoon over half the meat sauce. Add potatoes in a layer, sprinkle with another third of parmesan cheese, then spoon over remaining meat sauce, finish with a layer of eggplant.

Pour hot cheese sauce over eggplant, sprinkle with combined remaining parmesan cheese and crumbs. Bake in moderate oven for 1 hour.

Meat Sauce: Heat oil in large frying pan, add onion and garlic, cook, stirring, until onion is soft. Add mince, cook, stirring, until well browned. Stir in parsley, undrained crushed tomatoes, tomato paste, wine, oregano and cinnamon; bring to the boil, reduce heat, simmer, uncovered, for about 20 minutes or until liquid has evaporated. Process meat sauce in several batches until fine.

Cheese Sauce Layer: Melt butter in saucepan, stir in flour, cook for 1 minute; stir constantly. Gradually stir in milk, cream and nutmeg, stir constantly over heat until sauce boils and thickens. Remove from heat, stand 5 minutes, stir in cheese and egg.

Serves 6.

▶

EGGPLANT

▶ EGGPLANT IN COCONUT BATTER WITH TAMARIND SAUCE

Sauce can be made up to 2 days ahead. Recipe unsuitable to freeze or microwave.

2 medium eggplants
coarse cooking salt
cornflour
1 cup self-raising flour
⅔ cup water
½ cup coconut cream
2 eggs, lightly beaten
¾ cup coconut
oil for deep frying
TAMARIND DIPPING SAUCE
½ cup tamarind sauce
1 tablespoon water
1 teaspoon ground cumin
2 teaspoons sugar

Cut eggplants in half lengthways; slice thickly. Sprinkle with salt on both sides; stand 30 minutes. Rinse eggplant in water, drain, pat dry with absorbent paper.

Toss eggplant in cornflour, shake off excess cornflour. Sift self-raising flour into a large bowl, make well in centre, gradually stir in combined water, coconut cream and eggs, beat until smooth; stir in coconut.

Dip slices in batter, deep-fry slices a few at a time in hot oil until golden brown; drain on absorbent paper. Serve hot with sauce.

Tamarind Dipping Sauce: Combine all ingredients in bowl; mix well.

Serves 4.

Eggplant in Coconut Batter with Tamarind Sauce.

Plates & pot: Accoutrement; tiles: Pazotti

FENNEL

Fennel is also called Florence fennel and finocchio, and has been a favourite in the Mediterranean area since the times of ancient Romans. It was also a native of England, Wales and Ireland. To prepare: trim bulbs at top and base, remove hard core before using.

CREAM OF FENNEL SOUP

Recipe unsuitable to freeze.

30g butter
2 medium fennel bulbs, chopped
1 medium onion, chopped
1 medium apple, chopped
3 cups water
2 small chicken stock cubes,
   crumbled
2 teaspoons dried fennel seeds
1 cup milk

Melt butter in large frying pan, add fennel, onion and apple, cook, stirring, for 5 minutes (or microwave on HIGH for 5 minutes). Add water and stock cubes, bring to the boil, reduce heat, cover, simmer for 15 minutes (or microwave on HIGH for 5 minutes).

Toast fennel seeds on oven tray in moderate oven for 5 minutes, add to soup. Blend or process soup in several batches until smooth. Return soup to pan, add milk, reheat without boiling.

Serves 4.

CHEESY FENNEL LASAGNE

Lasagne can be assembled and frozen for up to 2 months.

1 medium fennel bulb, chopped
4 medium tomatoes, chopped
1 large carrot, grated
2 small zucchini, grated
1 medium onion, chopped
¼ cup tomato paste
1 clove garlic, crushed
1 teaspoon dried oregano leaves
200g packet instant lasagne noodles
¼ cup grated parmesan cheese
CHEESE SAUCE
30g butter
2 tablespoons plain flour
1½ cups milk
1½ cups grated tasty cheese
Combine fennel, tomatoes, carrot, zucchini, onion, tomato paste, garlic and oregano in large saucepan, cover, bring to the boil, reduce heat, simmer until vegetables are tender (or microwave on HIGH for about 10 minutes).

Layer lasagne noodles with cheese sauce and vegetable mixture in oven- ▶

ABOVE: Cream of Fennel Soup. BELOW: Cheesy Fennel Lasagne.

▶ proof dish, finishing with cheese sauce. Sprinkle with parmesan cheese, cover, bake in moderate oven for about 30 minutes (or microwave, covered, on HIGH for about 20 minutes) or until lasagne is tender. Remove lid, bake further 10 minutes or until brown.

Cheese Sauce: Melt butter in saucepan, add flour, cook, stirring, 1 minute. Gradually stir in milk, stir constantly over heat (or microwave on HIGH for about 3 minutes) or until mixture boils and thickens. Add cheese and stir until melted.

VEAL ROLLS WITH FENNEL

This recipe is unsuitable to freeze or microwave.

6 veal steaks (schnitzels)
3 medium fennel bulbs
2 bacon rashers, chopped
45g butter
1 medium onion, chopped
1 cup water
1 clove garlic, crushed
¼ cup chopped fresh parsley
¼ cup grated parmesan cheese
⅓ cup plain flour
2 tablespoons oil
1 tablespoon cornflour
1 small beef stock cube, crumbled
2 tablespoons brandy
2 teaspoons French mustard
¼ cup cream

Veal Rolls with Fennel.

Pound veal steaks until thin. Cut fennel into strips. Cook bacon in frying pan until just crisp, add half the butter and onion, cook, stirring, until onion is soft; add fennel, cook 5 minutes. Add a tablespoon of the water, garlic and 1 tablespoon of the parsley, cook 2 minutes. Sprinkle one side of each steak evenly with cheese, top with fennel mixture, roll up, secure with skewers. Toss rolls in flour. Heat oil and remaining butter in large frying pan, add rolls,

cook until golden brown, drain, place rolls in single layer in shallow ovenproof dish. Blend cornflour with remaining water and stock cube, add brandy and mustard, pour over rolls, cover, bake in moderate oven for about 1 hour or until rolls are tender. Baste and stir mixture several times during cooking time. Remove rolls, stir cream and remaining parsley into dish, serve sauce over rolls.

Serves 6.

FIGS

Figs originated in the Middle East and Mediterranean area. Mediterranean people were so dependent on figs and olives that the fig tree and olive branch symbolized peace and plenty. Figs are members of the mulberry family; some 700 varieties are believed to exist.

FIGS IN PINK CHAMPAGNE

Figs can be cooked up to 1 day ahead. Recipe unsuitable to freeze.

1 cup water
½ cup sugar
¼ cup lemon juice
2 cups pink champagne
8 medium figs, quartered

Combine water, sugar and lemon juice in saucepan, stir constantly over heat, without boiling, until sugar is dissolved (or microwave on HIGH for about 2 minutes).

Add figs, bring to the boil, reduce heat, simmer, uncovered, for 3 minutes (or microwave on HIGH about 2 minutes) or until figs are just tender. Remove from heat, cool to room tem-

Dish: Australian East India Co. lace cloth: Hampshire & Lowndes

perature, refrigerate until cold.

Serve figs in individual dishes topped with about ¼ cup of syrup. Top with champagne just before serving.

Serves 6.

FIG AND APPLE RELISH

Store relish in refrigerator for up to 6 weeks. This recipe is unsuitable to freeze or microwave.

10 medium figs, chopped
1 large onion, finely chopped
3 medium apples, finely chopped
2 cups brown sugar, firmly packed
1 cup sultanas
½ cup chopped dried apricots
2 cups white vinegar
1 cup dry white wine
¼ cup tomato paste
1 tablespoon yellow mustard seeds
1 clove garlic, chopped
½ teaspoon ground cinnamon
½ teaspoon ground cardamom

Combine all ingredients in large saucepan, stir constantly over heat, without boiling, until sugar is dissolved. Bring to the boil, reduce heat, simmer, uncovered, for about 1½ hours or until relish is as thick as desired. Stir mixture towards end of cooking time. Pour relish into hot sterilised jars and seal when cold.

Makes about 6 cups.

▶

China: Villeroy & Boch

ABOVE: Figs in Pink Champagne. LEFT: Fig and Apple Relish.

FIGS

Creamy Fig and Port Flan.

China: Mikasa

► CREAMY FIG AND PORT FLAN

Flan can be made up to one day ahead. Recipe unsuitable to freeze.

CRUMB CRUST
1½ cups plain sweet biscuit crumbs
90g butter, melted
FIG AND PORT FILLIING
500g figs, chopped
½ cup water
⅓ cup castor sugar
2 egg yolks
¼ cup castor sugar, extra

2 teaspoons cornflour
½ cup thickened cream
200g carton soft cream cheese
3 teaspoons gelatine
1½ tablespoons water, extra
2 tablespoons port

Crumb Crust: Combine crumbs and butter, press evenly over base and side of 23cm flan tin, refrigerate while making filling. Pour filling into crumb crust, refrigerate until set.

Fig and Port Filling: Combine figs, water and sugar in saucepan, bring to

the boil, reduce heat, simmer, covered, for 10 minutes (or microwave, covered, on HIGH for about 3 minutes).

Blend egg yolks, extra sugar and cornflour in saucepan, gradually stir in cream and cheese, stir constantly over heat until custard boils and thickens. Blend or process custard with fig mixture until smooth. Sprinkle gelatine over extra water, dissolve over hot water (or microwave on HIGH for about 20 seconds). Stir gelatine mixture and port into fig mixture.

GRAPEFRUIT

Different varieties of grapefruit came from East Asia, Polynesia and the West Indies. Commercial cultivation began in the late 19th century in Florida.

DELICIOUS GRAPEFRUIT PIE

This recipe is unsuitable to freeze or microwave.

CRUMB CRUST
1½ cups plain sweet biscuit crumbs
90g butter, melted
2 teaspoons grated grapefruit rind
RICH CREAM FILLING
5 eggs
⅔ cup castor sugar
1 cup grapefruit juice
125g butter, chopped
300ml carton thickened cream
TOPPING
300ml carton thickened cream
2 tablespoons castor sugar
1 small grapefruit
½ cup castor sugar, extra
¼ cup water

Crumb Crust: Combine all ingredients in bowl, mix well, press over base of 24cm greased springform tin. Pour filling into tin, bake in moderate oven for about 40 minutes or until set. Cool to room temperature; refrigerate several hours or overnight. Spread topping over filling, decorate with rind.

Rich Cream Filling: Combine eggs and sugar in top half of double saucepan or bowl over simmering water. Whisk until thick and creamy, add grapefruit juice and butter; whisk over water or until slightly thickened; cover; cool to room temperature. Fold in whipped cream in 2 batches.

Topping: Beat cream and sugar together until thick. Use vegetable peeler to remove rind thinly from grapefruit, cut rind into fine shreds. Combine extra sugar and water in saucepan, stir constantly over heat, without boiling, until sugar is dissolved. Bring to the boil, add grapefruit rind, simmer for about 3 minutes or until rind is soft and almost transparent. Drain rind, place on wire rack to cool.

▶

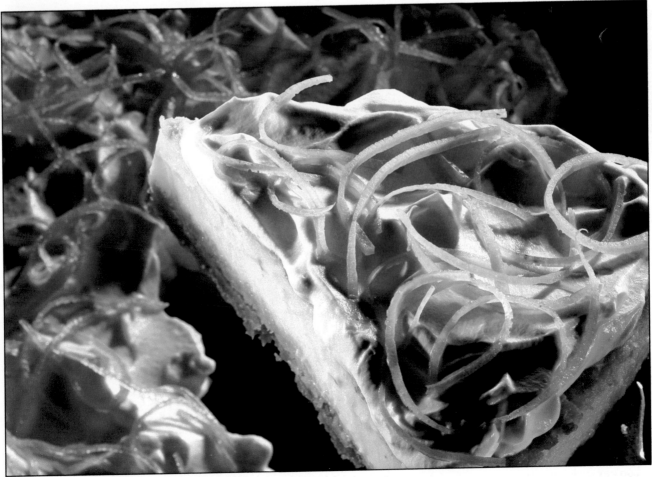

Delicious Grapefruit Pie.

GRAPEFRUIT

Grapefruit Mint Sorbet.

▶ GRAPEFRUIT MINT SORBET

½ cup sugar
1¼ cups water
2 cups grapefruit juice
2 tablespoons chopped fresh mint
2 egg whites

Combine sugar and water in saucepan, stir over heat, without boiling, until sugar is dissolved. Bring to the boil, reduce heat, simmer 10 minutes, uncovered, without stirring; cool. Add juice and mint to syrup, pour into lamington pan; cover with foil, freeze until partly set.

Process egg whites and juice mixture until smooth, pour back into lamington pan, cover, freeze overnight.

Serves 4.

Glasses: Hale Imports

PROCESSOR GRAPEFRUIT AND BRANDY MARMALADE

This recipe is unsuitable to freeze or microwave.

3 large grapefruit
4 cups (1 litre) water
6 cups (1½kg) sugar
⅓ cup brandy

Roughly chop grapefruit, seeds and all, then process or blend until finely chopped. Combine fruit and water in large saucepan or boiler, bring to the boil, reduce heat, simmer, covered, for 30 minutes. Transfer to large bowl, cover, stand overnight.

Next day, return mixture to boiler, bring to the boil and add sugar (mixture should not be more than 5cm deep at this stage). Stir until sugar is dissolved, without boiling, then boil rapidly, uncovered, without stirring, for about 20 minutes or until a teaspoon of jam jells when tested on a cold saucer. Stir in brandy, stand 5 minutes before pouring into hot sterilised jars; seal when cold.

Makes about 8 cups.

China: Mikasa

Processor Grapefruit and Brandy Marmalade.

GRAPES

Grapes were native to several areas including southern Europe, western Asia and parts of North Africa. The earliest records of wine production were in Egypt 6000 years ago.

GRAPE VINEGAR

As a dressing, use in the proportion of ⅔ cup oil to ⅓ cup grape vinegar. Vinegar will keep indefinitely. Recipe unsuitable to freeze or microwave.

500g black grapes
2 cups white vinegar
1 tablespoon sugar

▶ *Grape Vinegar.*

GRAPES

▶ Crush grapes in bowl with fork or potato masher. Add vinegar, cover, refrigerate 3 days. Strain mixture through fine cloth; discard pulp. Place grape liquid and sugar in saucepan, stir constantly over heat, without boiling, until sugar is dissolved. Pour into hot sterilised jars, seal when cold.

Makes about 2 cups.

LUSCIOUS GRAPE AND SOUR CREAM SHAPE

Recipe unsuitable to freeze.

2 cups clear grape juice
2 tablespoons sugar
2 x 200g cartons light sour cream
½ cup brown sugar
2 tablespoons gelatine
3 cups clear grape juice, extra
375g seedless white grapes

Combine grape juice and sugar in saucepan, stir constantly over heat, without boiling until sugar is dissolved.

Combine sour cream and brown sugar in separate bowl and leave at room temperature.

Sprinkle gelatine over extra grape juice, dissolve over hot water (or microwave on HIGH for 20 seconds); cool. Add 4 tablespoons of gelatine mixture to juice and sugar mixture. Reserve remaining gelatine mixture.

Divide juice and sugar mixture in half. Pour a thin layer from one half over base of lightly oiled 20cm ring pan, refrigerate until set.

Arrange half the grapes over jelly, pour remaining first half of juice and sugar mixture over grapes, refrigerate until set.

Add remaining gelatine mixture to sour cream mixture, spoon over first layer; refrigerate until set.

Finish with another layer of jelly, grapes and jelly.

GRAPE AND APPLE RELISH

Relish will keep in refrigerator for up to 6 weeks. This recipe is unsuitable to freeze or microwave.

1kg black grapes
1 cup dry white wine
2 cups water
3 whole cloves
2 tablespoons oil
2 medium onions, finely chopped
1 clove garlic, crushed
1 tablespoon grated fresh ginger
1 small fresh red chilli, chopped
4 medium apples, chopped
1 medium lemon, peeled, chopped
1 cup chopped dried figs
1 cup chopped raisins
⅓ cup brown sugar
1 cinnamon stick

ABOVE: Luscious Grape and Sour Cream Shape. LEFT: Grape and Apple Relish.

Combine grapes, wine, water and cloves in saucepan. Bring to boil, reduce heat, simmer, uncovered, 10 minutes. Strain, press as much liquid as possible from grapes, reserve liquid. Discard skins.

Heat oil in large saucepan, add onions, garlic, ginger and chilli, cook, stirring, 1 minute. Add apples, lemon, figs, raisins, sugar, cinnamon and reserved liquid, bring to boil, reduce heat, simmer 40 minutes or until as thick as desired.

Pour into hot sterilised jars, seal when cold. Store in refrigerator.

Makes about 5 cups.

KIWI FRUIT

Kiwi fruit
(Chinese
gooseberry)
is one of 40
species of
hardy
climbing
shrubs. Only
three species
produce
edible fruits;
they are
indigenous to
China. The
fruit was first
grown in New
Zealand in
1910. To
prepare: peel
with a knife or
vegetable
peeler.

KIWI FRUIT JAM

Citrus pectin is available from health food stores. Recipe unsuitable to freeze or microwave.

12 large kiwi fruit
½ teaspoon citrus pectin
2 tablespoons water
2 tablespoons lemon juice
2 cups sugar
green food colouring

Cut fruit into eighths, discard seeds and core. Blend or process pectin, water, lemon juice and 1 tablespoon of the sugar until smooth. Add kiwi fruit, process until they are roughly chopped (not smooth).

Combine kiwi fruit mixture and remaining sugar in large saucepan or boiler (mixture should not be more than 5cm deep at this stage). Stir constantly over heat, without boiling, until sugar is dissolved. Bring to the boil, boil rapidly, uncovered, without stirring, for about 10 minutes or until a teaspoon of mixture will jell when tested on a cold saucer. Tint with food colouring, if desired, mix well, allow bubbles to subside. Pour into hot sterilised jars, seal when cold.

Makes about 2½ cups. ▶

Kiwi Fruit Jam.

KIWI FRUIT

Mini Meringues with Kiwi Fruit and Liqueur Sauce.

Plate : Accoutrement

▶ MINI MERINGUES WITH KIWI FRUIT AND LIQUEUR SAUCE

Meringues can be made up to a week ahead; store in an airtight container when cold. If weather is humid or raining, store in refrigerator. Kirsch is a cherry-flavoured liqueur. This recipe is unsuitable to freeze or microwave.

3 egg whites
¾ cup castor sugar
1 teaspoon white vinegar
2 tablespoons chopped shredded coconut

300ml carton thickened cream
2 teaspoons icing sugar
2 medium kiwi fruit, sliced
KIWI FRUIT AND LIQUEUR SAUCE
2 medium kiwi fruit
1 teaspoon icing sugar
1 teaspoon Kirsch

Cover oven tray with foil, grease and dust with flour, shake off excess flour.

Beat egg whites in small bowl with electric mixer until soft peaks form, gradually add sugar, beat until dissolved, beat in vinegar. Spread meringue into 4 oval shapes on tray, allowing about 4cm between shapes; leave centres hollow. Sprinkle edges with coconut.

Bake in very slow oven for about 40 minutes or until meringues are dry and firm to touch. Turn oven off, leave meringues to cool in oven with door ajar.

Beat cream and sifted icing sugar together until firm; fill meringues with cream; top with kiwi fruit and sauce.
Kiwi Fruit and Liqueur Sauce: Blend or process ingredients until smooth; strain to remove seeds.

Makes 4.

KIWI FRUIT WATER ICE

Ice can be made up to 2 days in advance. This recipe is unsuitable to microwave.

8 medium kiwi fruit
1 cup sugar
1 cup water
1 cup dry white wine
1 cup water, extra

Blend or process kiwi fruit until smooth. Push pulp through sieve to remove seeds.

Place sugar and water in saucepan, stir constantly over heat, without boiling, until sugar is dissolved. Bring to the boil, boil rapidly 3 minutes, without stirring. Remove sugar syrup from heat, cool for 5 minutes; stir in kiwi fruit with remaining ingredients.

Pour into lamington pan, cover with foil; freeze until mixture is starting to set around edges of pan. Remove from freezer, mix well with a fork, cover; freeze overnight.

Serves 4 to 6.

Plate: Kosta Boda

Kiwi Fruit Water Ice.

LEEKS

Leeks are members of the onion family, and are believed to be native to the eastern Mediterranean area. The Romans introduced leeks to the British Isles. To prepare: cut off roots, trim green tops, leaving about 8cm of green part. Remove any damaged outer layers. Cut a couple of slits in top of leeks, soak leeks in warm water to loosen grit between leaves, rinse leeks in cold water.

TASTY LEEK PIE WITH AN EASY BREAD CASE

This recipe is unsuitable to freeze or microwave.

12 slices wholemeal bread
90g butter, melted
¾ cup grated tasty cheese
1 small red pepper, chopped

► *Tasty Leek Pie with An Easy Bread Case.*

LEEKS

Leek and Corn Chowder.

▶ LEEK AND PEPPER FILLING
30g butter
3 medium leeks, sliced
1 small red pepper, chopped
1 clove garlic, crushed
2 tablespoons cornflour
1 cup water
1 small chicken stock cube, crumbled
200g carton light sour cream
3 eggs, lightly beaten
pinch cayenne pepper

Remove crusts from bread. Brush bread with butter. Line base and side of pie plate with bread, buttered side down. Sprinkle cheese over base, press down firmly. Cut remaining bread slices into thin strips. Pour filling into pie plate, top with bread strips and pepper, bake in moderate oven for about 30 minutes or until set. Stand 5 minutes before cutting.

Leek and Pepper Filling: Melt butter in frying pan, add leeks, cook for about 15 minutes (or microwave on HIGH for about 5 minutes) or until soft, stir in pepper and garlic, cook 1 minute. Stir in blended cornflour and water with stock cube, stir constantly over heat (or microwave on HIGH for about 3 minutes)until mixture boils and thickens. Stir in sour cream, cool 5 minutes, stir in eggs and cayenne pepper.

LEEK AND CORN CHOWDER

Recipe unsuitable to freeze.

3 medium leeks, chopped
6 bacon rashers, chopped
1 medium kumara, chopped
1 medium potato, chopped
2 medium carrots, chopped
2 cups water

1 small chicken stock cube, crumbled
440g can corn kernels, drained
30g butter
¼ cup plain flour
1 cup milk

Combine leeks, bacon, kumara, potato, carrots, water and stock cube in large saucepan, cover, bring to the boil, reduce heat, simmer for about 25 minutes (or microwave on HIGH for about 10 minutes) or until vegetables are tender. Stir in corn.

Melt butter in small saucepan, add flour, cook for 1 minute, stirring constantly. Gradually stir in milk, stir constantly over heat (or microwave on HIGH for 3 minutes) or until mixture boils and thickens.

Stir into vegetable mixture, reheat before serving.

Serves 6.

LEEK AND TOMATO CASSEROLE

This recipe is unsuitable to freeze or microwave.

6 medium leeks
30g butter
1 tablespoon oil
1 clove garlic, crushed
425g can tomatoes
1 teaspoon sugar
30g butter, extra
1 cup stale breadcrumbs
¼ cup grated parmesan cheese
½ cup canned drained pimientos, chopped
½ cup black olives, chopped

Chop 1 leek finely; halve remaining leeks, place in greased ovenproof dish.

Heat butter and oil in frying pan, add chopped leek and garlic, cook 2 minutes, add undrained crushed tomatoes and sugar, bring to the boil, reduce heat, simmer, covered, 15 minutes. Pour tomato mixture over leeks in dish; bake, covered, in moderate oven 20 minutes.

Melt extra butter in saucepan, add breadcrumbs, stir until lightly browned, add cheese. Sprinkle mixture over leeks, top with pimientos and olives, bake further 5 minutes.

Serves 4.

Leek and Tomato Casserole.

LEMONS

The origin of the lemon is uncertain. It is most likely to have come from East India, Burma and South China. The Arabs did not cultivate the lemon until the 14th century.

LEMON MERINGUE PIE

This recipe is unsuitable to freeze or microwave.

PASTRY
2 cups plain flour
1 tablespoon icing sugar
185g butter
2 egg yolks, lightly beaten
1 tablespoon water, approximately

► *Lemon Meringue Pie.*

LEMONS

Plate: Village Living; cane table: Raw Straw

Chilli Tomato and Fish Salad.

until lightly browned. Stand 5 minutes before serving.

Lemon Filling: Combine cornflour and sugar in saucepan, gradually stir in lemon juice and water, stir until smooth. Stir constantly over heat until mixture boils and thickens. Reduce heat, simmer, stirring, 1 minute. Remove from heat, quickly stir in lemon rind, egg yolks and butter, stir until butter is melted, cover; cool to room temperature.

Meringue: Beat egg whites in small bowl with electric mixer until soft peaks form, gradually add sugar, beat until dissolved between each addition.

CHILLI TOMATO AND FISH SALAD

We used bream fillets in this recipe; the marinating of the fish takes the place of the cooking process. Recipe unsuitable to freeze or microwave.

500g white fish fillets, chopped
1½ cups lemon juice
1 teaspoon salt
1 medium tomato
1 medium green pepper, chopped
1 small fresh red chilli, finely
   chopped
2 green shallots, chopped
1 small cucumber, chopped
1½ cups tomato juice
1 teaspoon sugar

Combine fish, lemon juice and salt in large bowl, cover, refrigerate for about 2 hours or overnight (fish should be white and tender).

Wash fish in cold water; drain. Cut tomato in half, scoop out pulp, keep pulp for another use. Chop tomato shells, combine in bowl with fish, pepper, chilli, shallots, cucumber, tomato juice and sugar, cover; refrigerate for 1 hour before serving.

Serves 4.

LEMON BUTTER

Lemon butter can be made up to 4 weeks ahead; store in refrigerator. This recipe is unsuitable to freeze or microwave.

4 eggs
¾ cup sugar
2 teaspoons grated lemon rind
½ cup lemon juice
¼ cup water
125g butter, chopped

Combine all ingredients in top half of double saucepan or in heatproof bowl, stir constantly over simmering water until mixture thickly coats the back of a wooden spoon. Pour into hot sterilised jars; seal when cold.

Makes about 3 cups.

► LEMON FILLING
½ cup cornflour
1 cup sugar
½ cup lemon juice
1¼ cups water
2 teaspoons grated lemon rind
3 egg yolks
60g unsalted butter
MERINGUE
3 egg whites
½ cup castor sugar
Pastry: Sift flour and icing sugar into bowl, rub in butter, add egg yolks and

enough water to bind ingredients together. Cover, refrigerate pastry for 30 minutes.

Roll pastry large enough to line 23cm flan tin. Cover pastry with greaseproof paper, fill with dried beans or rice. Bake in moderately hot oven 7 minutes, remove paper and beans; bake further 7 minutes or until golden brown, cool to room temperature.

Spread filling into pastry case, spread with meringue. Bake in moderately hot oven for about 5 minutes or

Lemon Butter.

THE FACTS

This chart gives you up-to-date, easily digestible facts to help you get the most from the fascinating world of fruit and vegetables.

Most fruit and vegetables are available all year round these days. The chart indicates the season when they are at their peak and in plentiful supply. Fruit and vegetables are naturally at their best when freshly picked so choose produce without bruises, blemishes or cracks.

Most fresh produce is best kept in the refrigerator; the time it will keep depends on its condition at the time of purchase. Once fruit and vegetables are cut, their keeping time decreases, and the food should be covered to keep the cut surface moist, and prevent aromas in the refrigerator.

To give you a guide to the important nutritives in these foods, Rosemary Stanton has worked out a grading system based on the daily needs.

"EXCELLENT" means the food contains more than 70% of the daily needs in an average-sized serving.
"VERY GOOD" means more than 50%.
"GOOD" means more than 25%.
"USEFUL" means more than 16%.
"SOME" means more than 10%.
"SMALL" means less than 10%.

Research is constantly coming up with intriguing facts about fruit and vegetables; here we list some:

- Folate is a member of the B group Vitamins; it is found in leafy green vegetables.
- Pectin is one of the soluble fibres found mainly in apples and the rind of citrus fruit — marmalade is a great source! It helps control the body's sugar and cholesterol levels.
- Potassium, iron and magnesium are all minerals necessary for the body. Fruit and vegetables are especially rich in potassium; this helps balance the salt we eat.
- Dietary fibre comes in many different forms. The kinds of fibre in fruit and vegetables not only prevent constipation but also have the potential to help control blood sugar and cholesterol levels.
- Complex carbohydrates occur in vegetables and some fruit. They are often deficient in our diet and are the muscle cells' favourite fuel — vital for energy for exercise.
- Vitamin C is found only in fruit and vegetables. This vitamin is very important to our body, but is delicate. It has three enemies, heat, water and air, so the longer it is exposed to one, two or all three elements the more it deteriorates. It seems that flavour retention parallels vitamin retention.

All of the fruit and vegetables in this chart contain other vitamins and minerals in varying small quantities. Some of the vitamins they contain have other names which you may recognise more readily:

Vitamin A	. . . . carotene
Vitamin B₁	. . . . thiamin
Vitamin B₂	. . . . riboflavin
Vitamin B₃	. . . . niacin
Vitamin B₅	. . . . pantothenic acid
Vitamin C	. . . . ascorbic acid

FRUIT AND VEGETABLES	AT THEIR BEST	HOW TO SELECT	HOW TO STORE	NUTRITIONAL VALUE	KILOJOULE/CALORIE COUNT
APPLES	Autumn/Winter	Good colour, smooth skin.	Refrigerate in vented plastic bags.	• Good source of dietary fibre including pectin.	1 large apple (200g) contains 300kJ (72 cals).
APRICOTS	Summer	Plump, fairly soft, uniform colour.	Unwrapped in crisper of refrigerator.	• Good source of dietary fibre. • Useful amounts of potassium.	1 medium apricot (30g) contains 85kJ (20 cals).
ARTICHOKES (Globe)	Spring	Heavy, plump, good green colour, tightly closed leaves.	Refrigerate in vented plastic bags.	• Excellent source of Vitamin C and dietary fibre. • Useful amounts of potassium.	1 medium artichoke (375g) contains 120kJ (28 cals).
ASPARAGUS	Spring	Straight, firm, good-coloured stems.	Wrap stem ends in damp absorbent paper; refrigerate.	• Excellent source of Vitamin C. • Good source of dietary fibre. • Useful amounts of Vitamins B₁, B₂, potassium and iron.	6 medium asparagus spears contain 60kJ (14 cals).
AVOCADOS	Autumn/Winter	Ready to eat when they feel slightly soft when squeezed very gently.	Unwrapped in refrigerator.	• Good source of Vitamins E, B₆ and folate. • Useful amounts of Vitamin C and potassium. • Some Vitamins B₂ and B₃. • Avocados are unusual; they contain fat in the form of mono-unsaturated fatty acids which can help lower blood cholesterol levels. • Avocados do not contain cholesterol.	Half medium avocado (100g) contains 820kJ (196 cals).

FRUIT AND VEGETABLES	AT THEIR BEST	HOW TO SELECT	HOW TO STORE	NUTRITIONAL VALUE	KILOJOULE/ CALORIE COUNT
BANANAS	Summer to Autumn	Bright yellow to gold skin, well rounded.	Unwrapped, room temperature in a cool, airy place.	• Good source of dietary fibre, Vitamins C and B$_6$. • Useful source of potassium. • Some Vitamin B$_2$ and folate. • Small amounts of other B group vitamins. • Provide complex carbohydrate (sugar bananas give double the amount of regular varieties).	1 medium banana (150g) contains 370kJ (88 cals).
BEANS (French)	Summer	Long, firm, green and straight, easily snapped.	Refrigerate in vented plastic bags.	• Very good source of Vitamin C. • Useful amounts of folate and dietary fibre.	100g beans contain 30kJ (7 cals).
BEETROOT	Winter	Smooth, firm skin, good round shape, rich deep red colour.	Refrigerate unwrapped after tops have been cut off.	• Good source of folate and dietary fibre. • Useful amounts of Vitamin C. • Small amounts of potassium and iron.	1 medium beetroot (160g) contains 190kJ (45 cals).
BLUEBERRIES	Summer	Firm plump berries.	Cover, refrigerate.	• Good source of Vitamin C.	125g blueberries contain 295kJ (70 cals).
BROCCOLI	Autumn/ Winter	Green compact flower heads (no yellow).	Refrigerate in plastic bags.	• Excellent source of Vitamin C; an average serve provides more than 3 times the daily needs. • Very good source of folate. • Good source of Vitamins B$_2$, B$_5$ and dietary fibre. • Useful amounts of Vitamins E, B$_6$, potassium and iron.	100g broccoli contain 95kJ (23 cals).
BRUSSELS SPROUTS	Autumn/ Winter	Firm, uniform green colour, compact heads.	Unwrapped in crisper of refrigerator.	• Excellent source of Vitamin C; an average serve provides more than 3 times the daily needs. • Very good source of folate and dietary fibre. • Useful source of Vitamins B$_2$, B$_6$, E and potassium.	100g Brussels sprouts contain 110kJ (26 cals).
CABBAGES	Winter	Firm round heads, outer leaves strong in colour and not limp.	Trim, wrap in plastic wrap, refrigerate.	• Excellent source of Vitamin C; an average serve provides well over the daily needs. • Good source of folate. • Useful source of dietary fibre, potassium and Vitamin B$_6$.	100g cabbage contain 110kJ (26 cals).
CARROTS	Winter	Firm, well formed, orange in colour.	Uncovered in crisper of refrigerator.	• Exceptionally rich in Vitamin A; a large carrot provides about twice the daily needs. • Good source of dietary fibre. • Useful source of Vitamin C. • Some Vitamin B$_6$.	1 medium carrot (120g) contains 125kJ (30 cals).
CAULIFLOWER	Autumn/ Winter	Firm, white, compact heads; avoid wilted leaves.	Cut off outer leaves; store in plastic bags in refrigerator.	• Excellent source of Vitamin C; an average serve provides more than twice the daily needs. • Good source of dietary fibre. • Useful source of Vitamins B$_5$, B$_6$, folate and potassium. • Some Vitamin K.	100g cauliflower contain 55kJ (13 cals).
CELERY	All year	Fresh, unwilted leaves and stems easily snapped.	Refrigerate in plastic bag.	• Useful source of Vitamin C and potassium.	1 medium stick (80g) contains 30kJ (7 cals).
CHERRIES	Summer	Firm, bright, uniform-coloured fruit with green stems.	Refrigerate in vented plastic bags.	• Excellent source of Vitamin C. • Useful source of potassium and dietary fibre.	125g cherries contain 250kJ (60 cals).
CHOKOES	Autumn	Firm, pale green colour.	Uncovered in crisper of refrigerator.	• Good source of Vitamin C.	1 medium choko (100g) contains 115kJ (27 cals).

THE FACTS

FRUIT AND VEGETABLES	AT THEIR BEST	HOW TO SELECT	HOW TO STORE	NUTRITIONAL VALUE	KILOJOULE/ CALORIE COUNT
CORN	Summer	Buy in husks which look fresh and green, kernels should be plump, tender, milky and pale yellow.	Store in husks in plastic bags in refrigerator.	• Excellent source of dietary fibre. • Good source of Vitamins B_1 and C, folate, potassium, iron and complex carbohydrate. • Useful source of Vitamins A, B_2, B_5, B_6 and E.	1 cob of corn (275g) contains 485kJ (116 cals).
CUCUMBERS	Summer	Firm, dark green colour.	Uncovered in crisper of refrigerator.	• Good source of Vitamin C.	1 medium cucumber (280g) contains 120kJ (29 cals).
CUMQUATS	Winter	Firm, glossy, fine-textured skin.	Uncovered in crisper of refrigerator.	• Excellent source of Vitamin C. • Good source of dietary fibre.	100g cumquats contain 200kJ (48 cals).
CUSTARD APPLES	Winter	Large, uniform green colour, no cracks.	Refrigerate uncovered.	• Excellent source of Vitamin C. • Good source of dietary fibre. • Useful source of Vitamin B_6, magnesium and potassium. • Some Vitamin B_2 and complex carbohydrate.	100g custard apple contain 310kJ (74 cals).
EGGPLANT (Aubergine)	Winter	Dark purple to black colour, firm, glossy skin.	Uncovered in crisper of refrigerator.	• Very good source of Vitamin C. • Useful source of iron. • Some Vitamins A, B_2 and dietary fibre.	1 medium eggplant (320g) contains 200kJ (48 cals).
FENNEL	Winter/ Spring	Bulb white and crisp, avoid wilted leaves.	Uncovered in crisper of refrigerator.	• Good source of Vitamin C. • Some potassium and dietary fibre.	1 medium fennel bulb (300g) contains 85kJ (20 cals).
FIGS	Summer	Fully coloured, firm, with natural bloom.	Uncovered in crisper of refrigerator.	• Very good source of dietary fibre. • Some potassium.	1 medium fig (85g) contains 145kJ (35 cals).
GRAPEFRUIT	Winter/ Spring	Firm, heavy fruit, with smooth bright yellow skin.	Uncovered in crisper of refrigerator.	• Excellent source of Vitamins B_5 and C, half a medium grapefruit provides more than the day's needs. • Good source of dietary fibre.	Half medium grapefruit (195g) contains 88kJ (21 cals).
GRAPES	Summer	Smooth, plump fruit with natural bloom, stems are attached.	Refrigerate in vented plastic bags.	• Good source of Vitamin C and dietary fibre. • Some Vitamin B_6 and potassium.	125g grapes contain 355kJ (85 cals).
KIWI FRUIT (Chinese Gooseberries)	Winter/ Spring	Good shape, light to medium brown and furry; eat when slightly soft.	Uncovered in crisper of refrigerator.	• Excellent source of Vitamin C; one medium kiwi fruit provides twice the daily needs. • Some potassium and dietary fibre.	1 medium kiwi fruit (100g) contains 175kJ (40 cals).
LEEKS	All year	Crisp green leaves, firm white bulbs.	Refrigerate in plastic bags.	• Excellent source of Vitamin C. • Very good source of dietary fibre. • Good source of Vitamins A, B_6, E and potassium. • Useful source of Vitamins B_1, B_2, iron and magnesium.	1 medium leek (200g) contains 255kJ (61 cals).
LEMONS	Winter	Firm, heavy, good colour, fine-textured skin.	Refrigerate uncovered.	• Excellent source of Vitamin C. • Some dietary fibre.	1 medium lemon (180g) contains 115kJ (27 cals).
LIMES	Autumn/ Winter	Firm, heavy for their size.	Uncovered in crisper of refrigerator.	• Excellent source of Vitamin C. • Some dietary fibre.	1 medium lime (85g) contains 80kJ (19 cals).
LYCHEES	Summer	Full red in colour and leathery to touch.	Refrigerate in plastic bags or freeze in skin.	• Small quantities of dietary fibre, vitamins and minerals.	5 medium lychees (115g) contain 225kJ (54 cals).

FRUIT AND VEGETABLES	AT THEIR BEST	HOW TO SELECT	HOW TO STORE	NUTRITIONAL VALUE	KILOJOULE/ CALORIE COUNT
MANDARINS	Winter	Firm, heavy, glossy orange skin.	Refrigerate uncovered.	• Excellent source of Vitamin C. • Some dietary fibre.	1 medium mandarin (105g) contains 200kJ (48 cals).
MANGOES	Summer	Good coloured, bright orange-yellow skins, deep pink blush.	Wrapped in refrigerator.	• Excellent source of Vitamins A and C. • Good source of dietary fibre. • Useful source of Vitamins B_1, B_6 and potassium.	1 medium mango (240g) contains 425kJ (102 cals).
MELONS	Summer to Autumn	Firm, heavy, good colour and aroma.	Refrigerate uncovered.	• Excellent source of Vitamin C. • Good source of folate. • Some potassium and dietary fibre. • Rockmelon is a useful source of Vitamin A.	200g melon contain 210kJ (50 cals).
MUSHROOMS	All year	Firm, unbroken caps, white or creamy.	Refrigerate in paper or calico bags or wrapped in absorbent paper.	• Good source of Vitamins B_2, B_3, B_5. • Useful source of Vitamin B_{12}, folate, potassium and dietary fibre.	100g mushrooms contain 55kJ (13 cals).
NECTARINES	Summer	Smooth, plump, highly coloured.	Refrigerate uncovered.	• Good source of Vitamin C. • Some Vitamin B_3, potassium and dietary fibre.	1 large nectarine (180g) contains 355kJ (85 cals).
ORANGES	Summer and Winter	Firm, heavy for their size.	Refrigerate uncovered.	• Excellent source of Vitamin C; one medium orange will provide more than twice the daily needs. • Good source of folate and dietary fibre. • Some Vitamin B_1 and potassium.	1 large orange (220g) contains 250kJ (60 cals).
PASSIONFRUIT	Summer to Autumn	Full, heavy fruit with smooth, dark purple skin.	Refrigerate in plastic bags.	• Excellent source of dietary fibre. • Good source of Vitamin C. • Some Vitamin B_3.	1 medium passionfruit (55g) contains 45kJ (11 cals).
PEACHES	Summer	Firm, good colour.	Refrigerate uncovered.	• Good source of Vitamin C. • Some Vitamin B_3, potassium and dietary fibre.	1 medium peach (150g) contains 205kJ (49 cals).
PEARS	Autumn	Good colour, slightly soft in stem area.	Refrigerate uncovered.	• Very good source of dietary fibre.	1 medium pear (150g) contains 250kJ (60 cals).
PEPPERS (Capsicums)	Summer	Well shaped, thick and firm, deep coloured glossy skin.	Uncovered in crisper of refrigerator.	• One of the richest sources of Vitamin C; one green pepper provides about 4 times the daily needs, and a red pepper twice as much as the green pepper. • Very good source of Vitamin A. • Good source of dietary fibre. • Some potassium.	1 medium pepper (150g) contains 100kJ (24 cals).
PINEAPPLES	Summer	Green colour with golden colour showing through, aroma is sweet.	Refrigerate uncovered.	• Very good source of Vitamin C.	150g pineapple contain 245kJ (59 cals).
PLUMS	Summer	Plump, bright fruit with smooth skin.	Refrigerate uncovered.	• Useful source of dietary fibre.	1 medium plum (70g) contains 110kJ (26 cals).
PUMPKINS	Summer/ Autumn	Feel heavy for their size.	Uncovered in crisper of refrigerator.	• Excellent source of Vitamins A and C. • Useful source of potassium and dietary fibre. • Some Vitamin E and iron.	100g pumpkin contain 51kJ (12 cals).
RASPBERRIES	Summer	Firm and dry, rich in colour with natural bloom.	Cover, refrigerate.	• One of the best sources of dietary fibre. • Excellent source of Vitamin C. • Useful quantities of iron, potassium and magnesium.	125g raspberries contain 130kJ (31 cals).
RHUBARB	Summer	Firm red stems, avoid wilted leaves.	Refrigerate uncovered.	• Good source of Vitamin C and fibre. • Useful source of Vitamin B_1. • Some Vitamin B_3.	1 cup chopped rhubarb (85g) contains 22kJ (5 cals).

▶

THE FACTS

FRUIT AND VEGETABLES	AT THEIR BEST	HOW TO SELECT	HOW TO STORE	NUTRITIONAL VALUE	KILOJOULE/ CALORIE COUNT
SHALLOTS (Golden)	Autumn/ Winter/ Spring	Well-formed, heavy for their size.	Cool, dry, airy place.	● Some Vitamin C.	1 medium shallot (15g) contains 45kJ (11 cals).
SNOW PEAS (Chinese peas, mange-tout)	Winter/ Spring	Firm, bright green pods without prominent peas.	Refrigerate in plastic bags.	● Excellent source of Vitamin C. ● Good source of potassium and dietary fibre. ● Useful amounts of Vitamins B_5, B_6, iron and magnesium.	100g snow peas contain 160kJ (38 cals).
SPINACH (English)	Autumn to Spring	Good green colour, avoid wilted leaves.	Uncovered in crisper of refrigerator.	● Excellent source of Vitamin C and folate. ● Very good source of Vitamin A. ● Good source of Vitamins B_2, E and potassium.	100g spinach (20 leaves) contain 80kJ (19 cals).
STRAWBERRIES	Spring	Good bright colour.	Cover, refrigerate in crisper.	● Excellent source of Vitamin C; 125g provide twice the daily needs. ● Some folate and dietary fibre.	125g strawberries contain 135kJ (32 cals).
TAMARILLOS (Tree Tomatoes)	Autumn/ Winter	Smooth, good colour, firm, stems intact.	Refrigerate uncovered.	● Good source of Vitamin C and dietary fibre. ● Some Vitamin A.	1 medium tamarillo (75g) contains 80kJ (19 cals).
TOMATOES	Summer	Firm, plump and red.	Uncovered in crisper of refrigerator.	● Excellent source of Vitamin C; a medium tomato provides the day's needs. ● Good source of Vitamin E, folate and dietary fibre. ● Some Vitamin A and potassium.	1 medium tomato (100g) contains 90kJ (22 cals).
ZUCCHINI	Summer	Firm, glossy skin, well shaped.	Refrigerate in plastic bags.	● Excellent source of Vitamin C.	1 medium zucchini (150g) contains 90kJ (22 cals).

LIMES

Limes probably originated in tropical Asia, possibly in the East Indies. The Arabs are most likely to have begun the distribution of this fruit into India and Persia. They are now grown in many tropical countries.

TANGY LIME AND SEAFOOD RICE

You will need 6 to 8 medium limes. This recipe is unsuitable to freeze or microwave.

2 tablespoons oil
1 clove garlic, crushed
1 medium onion, chopped
2 cups long grain rice
1 tablespoon grated lime rind
1½ cups water
1 small chicken stock cube, crumbled
½ cup lime juice
¼ cup dry white wine
500g uncooked mussels
500g uncooked king prawns
250g squid

2 tablespoons oil, extra
½ teaspoon chilli powder
2 teaspoons grated lime rind, extra
1 cup water, extra

Heat oil in large saucepan, add garlic and onion, cook, stirring, until onion is soft. Add rice, stir until rice is coated with oil. Combine lime rind, water, stock cube, lime juice and wine, add to the rice mixture. Bring rice mixture to the boil, reduce heat, simmer, covered, 25 minutes or until stock is absorbed and rice is tender.

Clean mussels. Shell and devein prawns, leaving tails intact. Clean squid, cut into rings.

Heat extra oil in frying pan, add chilli powder and extra lime rind, cook, stirring, 1 minute. Add prawns and squid,

cook, stirring, until seafood is tender.

Remove from pan, add mussels and extra water. Cover, cook 2 minutes or until mussels are open. Add mussels to seafood mixture, discard any that do not open; stir through rice.

Serves 6.

LIME GINGER MARMALADE

Marmalade can be stored for up to 12 months in the refrigerator. This recipe is unsuitable to freeze or microwave.

6 large limes
6 cups water
7 cups sugar, approximately
2 teaspoons finely grated fresh
**   ginger**

Slice limes thinly, remove and discard seeds. Combine limes in bowl with water, cover, stand overnight.

Next day, transfer mixture to large boiler, bring to boil, reduce heat, simmer, covered, about 1 hour or until rind is tender.

Measure fruit mixture, allow 1 cup sugar to each 1 cup of fruit mixture. Return fruit mixture and sugar to boiler (mixture should not be more than 5cm deep at this stage), stir without boiling over high heat until sugar is dissolved. Bring to the boil, boil rapidly, uncovered, without stirring, about 15 minutes or until a teaspoon of mixture jells ▶

ABOVE: Tangy Lime and Seafood Rice. LEFT: Lime Ginger Marmalade.

LIMES

▶ when tested on a cold saucer.

Remove boiler from heat, add ginger, stand 10 minutes before pouring into hot sterilised jars; seal when cold.

Makes about 8 cups.

LIME DELICIOUS PUDDINGS

You will need about 4 small limes for this recipe. Puddings are unsuitable to freeze or microwave.

30g butter
½ cup castor sugar
2 eggs, separated
2 tablespoons self-raising flour
¼ cup lime juice
¼ cup water
¾ cup milk

Cream butter, sugar and egg yolks together in small bowl with electric mixer until light and creamy. Stir in sifted flour, juice, water and milk. Beat egg whites until soft peaks form, gently fold through mixture. Pour into 6 lightly greased ovenproof dishes (half cup capacity). Bake in moderately slow oven 35 minutes.

Serves 6.

Lime Delicious Puddings.

Soufflé pots: Inini

LYCHEES

Lychees are natives of Southern China, and have been cultivated there for more than 2000 years. To prepare: peel away skins with fingers, carefully remove stones before using.

Crispy Pork with Lychee Sweet and Sour Sauce.

China: Made Where

Poached Lychees with Orange Sabayon.

CRISPY PORK WITH LYCHEE SWEET AND SOUR SAUCE

This recipe is unsuitable to freeze or microwave.

750g pork fillet
2 tablespoons oil
¼ cup dry sherry
2 teaspoons light soya sauce
2 cloves garlic, crushed
2 teaspoons grated fresh ginger
1 egg, lightly beaten
¾ cup cornflour
oil for deep frying
1 tablespoon oil, extra
1 medium onion, coarsely chopped
1 medium red pepper, chopped
1 clove garlic, crushed, extra
1 tablespoon cornflour, extra
¾ cup canned pineapple juice

1 cup water
2 teaspoons white vinegar
1 tablespoon hoisin sauce
750g fresh lychees, chopped
4 green shallots, chopped

Cut pork into bite-sized pieces, combine in large bowl with oil, sherry, soya sauce, garlic and ginger, cover, refrigerate 2 hours or overnight. Stir egg and cornflour into pork mixture. Deep-fry pork pieces in hot oil, about 10 at a time, until pork is golden brown and tender, drain on absorbent paper. Repeat with remaining pork.

Heat extra oil in frying pan or wok, add onion, pepper and extra garlic, stir in blended extra cornflour and pineapple juice, water, vinegar and hoisin sauce, stir constantly over heat until mixture boils and thickens. Add pork

and lychees, stir until heated through. Serve sprinkled with shallots.

Serves 4.

POACHED LYCHEES WITH ORANGE SABAYON

Recipe unsuitable to freeze.

1kg fresh lychees
2 tablespoons castor sugar
1 tablespoon water
½ teaspoon grated orange rind
2 tablespoons orange juice
1 tablespoon marsala
4 egg yolks
⅓ cup castor sugar, extra
1 teaspoon vanilla essence

Combine lychees, sugar, water, orange rind and juice and marsala in saucepan. Stir constantly over heat, without ▶

China: Mikasa; napkin: Modern Living

LYCHEES

▶ boiling, until sugar is dissolved. Bring to the boil, reduce heat, simmer, covered, 10 minutes, drain; reserve quarter cup of liquid.

Whisk egg yolks and extra sugar together in top half of double saucepan or in heatproof bowl over simmering water; whisk constantly (or beat with rotary beater or electric mixer) for about 10 minutes. Gradually whisk in reserved liquid and essence, whisk until mixture thickens. Remove from heat; serve over lychees.

Serves 4.

LYCHEE SUNRISE COCKTAIL

Recipe unsuitable to freeze.

2 cups orange juice
grenadine syrup
500g fresh lychees
1½ teaspoons sugar
⅓ cup gin
12 ice cubes
1 tablespoon lime juice

Divide orange juice evenly between 4 large glasses. Pour a few drops of grenadine into juice; stir once to give marbled effect. Blend or process lychees, sugar, gin, ice and lime juice until smooth. Carefully pour lychee mixture over orange juice.

Serves 4.

Glasses & mats: Made Where

Lychee Sunrise Cocktail.

MANDARINS

Mandarins are sometimes called tangerines (which are another variety along with tangelos). They originated in China, and are also found in the Philippines. To prepare: peel skin and separate fruit into segments.

MANDARIN BAVAROIS

Bavarois can be made a day ahead. This recipe is unsuitable to freeze or microwave.

SPONGE
1 egg
1½ tablespoons castor sugar
1 teaspoon vanilla essence
2 tablespoons self-raising flour
300ml carton thickened cream
½ cup chopped pecans or walnuts
2 medium mandarins, segmented
BAVAROIS
3 egg yolks
½ cup castor sugar
¼ cup milk
¾ cup mandarin juice
3 teaspoons gelatine
300ml carton thickened cream
JELLY
1½ teaspoons gelatine
½ cup mandarin juice
1 teaspoon sugar

Sponge: Grease base and side of 20cm sandwich pan, line base with paper, grease paper.

Beat egg, sugar and essence together in small bowl with electric mixer until thick and pale. Fold in sifted flour, spread into prepared pan. Bake in moderate oven for about 10 minutes. Cool to room temperature.

Place sponge into 20cm springform tin, pour bavarois over sponge, refrigerate about 1 hour or until set. Pour jelly evenly over bavarois, refrigerate until set. Remove dessert from tin to serving plate, spread some of the whipped cream around the side, press nuts onto cream. Decorate with remaining cream and mandarin segments.

Bavarois: Combine egg yolks and sugar in small bowl, beat with electric

72

Mandarin Bavarois.

mixer until thick and creamy. Heat milk in saucepan, gradually pour into egg mixture while beating constantly.

Place mixture into saucepan, stir constantly over heat, without boiling, until mixture thickens slightly, strain;

add half cup of the mandarin juice. Sprinkle gelatine over remaining mandarin juice, dissolve over hot water, stir into custard mixture. Refrigerate until set to the consistency of unbeaten egg white; fold in whipped cream.

Jelly: Sprinkle gelatine over quarter cup of the mandarin juice, dissolve over hot water (or microwave on HIGH for about 15 seconds). Stir in sugar and remaining mandarin juice, cool jelly until slightly thickened before using. ▶

MANDARINS

▶ MANDARIN CHICKEN SALAD

Recipe unsuitable to freeze.

4 chicken breast fillets
2 tablespoons honey
1 tablespoon light soya sauce
1 teaspoon grated fresh ginger
1 teaspoon grated mandarin rind
¼ cup mandarin juice
1 lettuce
1 cup bean sprouts
125g baby mushrooms, sliced
2 medium mandarins, segmented
4 green shallots, chopped
SESAME MANDARIN DRESSING
⅓ cup oil
1 teaspoon sesame oil
½ teaspoon grated mandarin rind
¼ cup mandarin juice
1 teaspoon sugar
1 clove garlic, crushed
pinch five spice powder

Combine chicken, honey, soya sauce, juice squeezed from ginger (do this between 2 teaspoons), mandarin rind and juice in ovenproof dish. Cover, refrigerate several hours or overnight.

Bake chicken, covered, in moderate oven 20 minutes (or microwave on HIGH for about 10 minutes) or until chicken is tender, cool. Serve chicken sliced with remaining ingredients; top with dressing just before serving.

Sesame Mandarin Dressing: Combine all ingredients in jar, shake well.

Serves 4.

MANDARIN JELLY

This recipe is unsuitable to freeze or microwave.

15 medium mandarins
1 cup lemon juice
8 cups (2 litres) water
8 cups (2kg) sugar

Squeeze juice from mandarins, pour into large saucepan or boiler; add pulp, lemon juice and water. Bring to boil, reduce heat, simmer, covered, for 1 hour. Strain mixture through a fine cloth into a bowl. Allow liquid to drip through cloth slowly; do not squeeze or press pulp as this will make a cloudy jelly; discard pulp.

Return mandarin liquid to clean pan, bring to boil, add sugar (mixture should not be more than 5cm deep at this stage), stir constantly over heat, without boiling, until sugar is dissolved. Bring to boil, boil rapidly, uncovered, without stirring, for about 30 minutes or until the jelly sets when tested on a cold saucer.

Makes about 5 cups.

ABOVE LEFT: Mandarin Chicken Salad. LEFT: Mandarin Jelly.

MANGOES

Mangoes originated in the East Indies and Malaya. They have been cultivated for more than 4000 years in India. To prepare: peel skin before using.

MANGO CHICKEN

This recipe is unsuitable to freeze or microwave.

2 tablespoons slivered almonds
4 chicken breast fillets
2 tablespoons cornflour
15g butter
1 tablespoon oil
1 medium onion, finely chopped
1 clove garlic, crushed
2 large mangoes, chopped
1 teaspoon grated lime rind
1 tablespoon castor sugar
1 teaspoon cornflour, extra
½ cup water
1 small chicken stock cube,
  crumbled
2 tablespoons lime juice
2 green shallots, finely chopped

Toast nuts on oven tray in moderate oven for about 5 minutes, cool.

Cut each fillet into 4, toss in cornflour. Heat butter and oil in frying pan, add chicken gradually to pan in single layer, stir constantly over heat until chicken is well-browned all over. Add onion and garlic to pan, cook until onion is soft; add mangoes, rind and sugar, cook 1 minute. Stir in blended extra cornflour, water, stock cube and lime juice; bring to the boil, stirring constantly, reduce heat, simmer, uncovered, 5 minutes. Serve chicken sprinkled with shallots and almonds.

Serves 4.

MANGO AND PORT CHUTNEY

Chutney can be kept for up to 12 months; store in refrigerator. Recipe unsuitable to freeze or microwave. ▶

Mango Chicken.

MANGOES

▶ **4 medium mangoes, chopped**
¾ cup port
2 large onions, chopped
1 cup chopped raisins
2 teaspoons grated fresh ginger
2 small fresh red chillies, finely chopped
2 cups sugar
3 cups brown vinegar
2 teaspoons yellow mustard seeds

Combine mangoes in large saucepan or boiler with remaining ingredients, stir constantly over heat without boiling until sugar is dissolved. Bring to the boil; reduce heat, simmer, uncovered, for about 1½ hours or until chutney is thick. Chutney will need to be stirred occasionally towards the end of cooking time. Pour into hot, sterilised jars; seal when cold.

Makes about 5 cups.

MANGO CHEESECAKE

Cheesecake can be made up to a day ahead. Recipe unsuitable to freeze.

CRUMB CRUST
1 cup plain sweet biscuit crumbs
1 cup finely chopped pecans or walnuts
75g butter, melted
CREAM CHEESE FILLING
250g packet cream cheese
½ cup castor sugar

ABOVE: Mango Cheesecake. LEFT: Mango and Port Chutney.

3 medium mangoes, chopped
300ml carton thickened cream
1 tablespoon gelatine
¼ cup water
Crumb Crust: Combine crumbs, nuts and butter in bowl, mix well. Press evenly over base of greased 20cm springform tin, refrigerate 30 minutes. Pour filling over biscuit base, refrigerate several hours or until set.

Cream Cheese Filling: Process cream cheese, sugar and half the mango until smooth, add cream, process until combined. Transfer mixture to large bowl. Sprinkle gelatine over water, dissolve over hot water (or microwave on HIGH for about 30 seconds); cool, do not allow the mixture to set. Add gelatine to mango mixture; stir in the remaining mangoes.

MELONS

Melons belong to the same family as cucumbers, marrows and squash. They originated in the Middle East, probably Persia.

MELON AND RED CURRANT COCKTAIL

Maraschino is a cherry-flavoured liqueur. Serve this cocktail as a first course. Recipe unsuitable to freeze.

1 small honeydew melon
RED CURRANT SYRUP
⅓ cup red currant jelly
1 teaspoon grated orange rind
¾ cup orange juice
1 teaspoon French mustard
2 tablespoons maraschino
2 tablespoons port

Scoop small balls from melon, place in bowl, add syrup, cover, refrigerate for at least 1 hour before serving.

Red Currant Syrup: Place jelly in small saucepan, stir constantly over low heat until jelly is melted (or microwave on HIGH for about 2 minutes); stir in remaining ingredients.

Serves 4.

▶

Glass dish: Dansab

Melon and Red Currant Cocktail.

MELONS

Plate: Dansab

MELON STRAWS WITH ROCKMELON CREAM

Recipe unsuitable to freeze.

½ **medium rockmelon**
½ **medium honeydew melon**
¼ **small watermelon**
ROCKMELON CREAM
¼ **medium rockmelon**
½ **cup thickened cream**
½ **cup sour cream**
2 **tablespoons castor sugar**
½ **cup lightly packed mint leaves**

Cut melons into strips. Serve with rockmelon cream.

Rockmelon Cream: Blend or process melon until smooth, add cream, sour cream, sugar and mint, blend until mint is finely chopped.

Serves 6.

MELON SORBET

Use any melon of your choice. Recipe unsuitable to microwave.

400g **melon flesh**
½ **cup sugar**
1 **cup water**
2 **egg whites**

Blend or process melon until smooth; you need 2 cups purée.

Combine sugar and water in sauce-

Glass dish: Dansab

pan, stir constantly over heat, without boiling, until sugar is dissolved. Bring to the boil, reduce heat, simmer, uncovered, 10 minutes, without stirring; cool to room temperature. Stir melon purée into sugar syrup, pour

into lamington pan, cover with foil, freeze until partly set.

Process egg whites and melon mixture until smooth, pour back into pan, cover, freeze overnight.

Serves 4.

ABOVE: Melon Sorbet. LEFT: Melon Straws with Rockmelon Cream.

MUSHROOMS

Mushrooms are not a vegetable, but belong to the fungi family. The French were first to cultivate them commercially. To prepare: cultivated mushrooms simply need wiping with a damp cloth; use stems and caps. For field mushrooms, cut away thick stems and peel caps.

MUSHROOM PEPPER SAUCE

You will need to cook 250g pasta for this recipe; Sauce unsuitable to freeze or microwave.

1 tablespoon oil
1 clove garlic, crushed
1 medium red pepper, sliced
1 medium green pepper, sliced
750g baby mushrooms
¼ cup dry red wine
2 teaspoons Worcestershire sauce
1 tablespoon chopped fresh parsley

Heat oil in saucepan, add garlic and peppers, cook until peppers are just tender. Add mushrooms, cook 1 minute; add wine, sauce, parsley; cover, simmer 5 minutes. Serve over pasta.
  Serves 2. ▶

Mushroom Pepper Sauce.

Serving ware: Villa Italiana; linen: Australian East India Co.

Mushrooms

▶ MUSHROOM AND PATE OMELET

Use canned, ready-made or home-made pâté or a good liverwurst. Recipe unsuitable to freeze or microwave.

1 slice bread
30g butter
200g baby mushrooms, sliced
30g pâté
1 green shallot, chopped
OMELET
2 eggs
2 teaspoons water
1 teaspoon butter

Remove crusts from bread, cut bread into small cubes. Toast on oven tray in moderate oven for about 10 minutes.

Melt butter in frying pan, add mushrooms, cook until tender, stir in pâté and shallot, stir over heat until pâté is melted. Serve spooned over omelet, sprinkle with bread cubes.

Omelet: Beat eggs and water together with fork in bowl. Heat 20cm frying pan, add butter. When butter is melted, pour in egg mixture. Before omelet sets, use a spatula to pull edges towards centre to allow uncooked liquid to run underneath omelet. Tilt pan over heat until eggs are just set; top should still be creamy. Carefully fold omelet in half, slide onto plate.

Serves 1.

MUSHROOM ALMOND TERRINE

Terrine can be made 4 days ahead; it is unsuitable to freeze or microwave.

30g butter
1kg mushrooms, sliced
2 cloves garlic, crushed
2 tablespoons port
¾ cup blanched almonds
3 eggs, lightly beaten
½ cup thickened cream
1½ cups (180g) grated tasty cheese
8 bacon rashers

Heat butter in large frying pan, add mushrooms, cook over high heat, stirring constantly, until lightly browned. Add garlic and port, cook 1 minute, remove from heat, place in colander over bowl; cool.

Toast almonds on oven tray in moderate oven 5 minutes. Combine eggs, cream and cheese in large bowl, add cooled drained mushrooms and nuts.

Line a 14cm x 21cm loaf pan with bacon, pour mushroom mixture into pan. Fold ends of bacon over filling, cover with greaseproof paper, tie paper around rim of pan with string. Place terrine in baking dish with enough boiling water to come halfway up sides of pan. Bake in moderate oven 1½ hours, remove from dish, cool, refrigerate overnight.

ABOVE: Mushroom and Pâté Omelet. BELOW: Mushroom Almond Terrine.

NECTARINES

Nectarines are linked with peaches in history, and are believed to have come from China. The name nectarine is believed to have come from the Greek "nekter", meaning drink of the gods. To remove the skin, place nectarines into bowl, add enough boiling water to cover; drain immediately, and peel skin.

Poached Nectarines with Almond Cream Custard.

Plate: Village Living

POACHED NECTARINES WITH ALMOND CREAM CUSTARD

Nectarines can be prepared up to a week ahead and custard up to 3 days ahead. This recipe is unsuitable to freeze or microwave.

2 cups water
1 cup dry white wine
1 cup lemonade
1 cup sugar
1 cinnamon stick
2 tablespoons brandy
8 medium nectarines, halved
2 tablespoons flaked almonds
ALMOND CREAM CUSTARD
2 tablespoons castor sugar
2 egg yolks
¾ cup milk
½ teaspoon almond essence
1 teaspoon cornflour
1 teaspoon water
2 tablespoons cream

Combine water, wine, lemonade and sugar in saucepan, stir constantly over heat, without boiling, until sugar is dissolved. Bring to boil, add cinnamon stick, brandy and nectarines. Reduce heat, simmer, uncovered, 5 minutes. Remove from heat, stand 10 minutes, remove nectarines, peel nectarines and return to sugar syrup, refrigerate.

Toast almonds on oven tray in moderate oven 5 minutes. Pour thin layer of custard onto serving plates. Drain nectarines, pat dry with absorbent paper, cut into fan shapes. Place onto plates, top with toasted almonds.

Almond Cream Custard: Place sugar and egg yolks in small bowl, beat with electric mixer until thick and creamy. Combine milk and essence in saucepan, bring to boil, remove from heat, stir into egg mixture. Return mixture to saucepan, stir constantly over low heat, without boiling, until custard thickens slightly. Stir in blended cornflour and water, stir constantly over heat until custard boils and thickens. Add cream, cool; refrigerate.

Serves 4.

NECTARINE AND WINE JELLIES

Jellies can be made up to 2 days ahead. This recipe is unsuitable to freeze or microwave.

1 medium orange
1½ cups water
⅔ cup dry white wine
¾ cup sugar
1½kg nectarines, chopped
10 fresh mint leaves
3 teaspoons gelatine

Using a vegetable peeler, remove 2 strips of rind from orange. Combine water, wine, sugar and rind in large saucepan, bring to boil, reduce heat, simmer, uncovered, for 3 minutes; ▶

NECTARINES

Nectarine and Prawn Salad with Orange Dressing.

Bowl & decanter: H.A.G.; tiles: Northbridge Ceramic & Marble Centre

▶ discard rind. Add nectarines and mint to sugar syrup, bring to boil, reduce heat, simmer for about 3 minutes or until nectarines are just tender, stirring occasionally. Strain into bowl, reserve 2½ cups sugar syrup; discard mint.

Sprinkle gelatine over half the sugar syrup, dissolve over hot water, cool to room temperature; do not allow to set. Add gelatine mixture to remaining sugar syrup.

Divide nectarines evenly into 6 dishes (1¼ cup capacity). Pour gelatine mixture evenly into dishes, cover, refrigerate the jellies for about 2 hours or until set.

Makes 6.

NECTARINE AND PRAWN SALAD WITH ORANGE DRESSING

Recipe unsuitable to freeze.

1kg nectarines, sliced
1kg cooked prawns, shelled
1 small bunch endive
2 witlof (chicory)
250g honey snap peas (or snow peas)
5 green shallots, chopped
3 green cucumbers
5 spring onions, sliced
ORANGE DRESSING
¾ cup orange juice
2 tablespoons cider vinegar
2 tablespoons oil
1 tablespoon brown sugar
Combine nectarines, prawns, endive, witlof, peas, shallots, cucumbers and onions in bowl, add dressing just before serving.

Orange Dressing: Combine all ingredients in jar; shake well.

Serves 6.

Nectarine and Wine Jellies.

ORANGES

Oranges originated in China, and were introduced into Spain by the Arabs. The orange was known to the Romans, and was cultivated widely around the Mediterranean area during the period of the Arab empire. Now it is found in many varieties throughout the world.

ORANGE CREPES

Crêpes can be made the day before required. Spread with marmalade and cook in sauce just before serving. Grand Marnier is an orange-flavoured liqueur. Unfilled crêpes can be frozen for up to 6 months. Recipe unsuitable to microwave.

½ cup marmalade
60g unsalted butter
¼ cup castor sugar
1 tablespoon grated orange rind
½ cup orange juice

▶

ORANGES

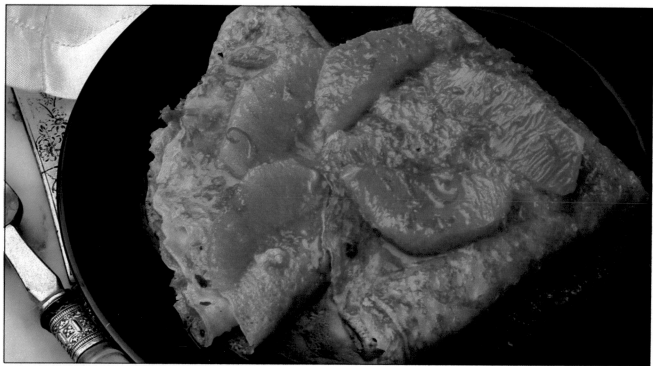

Orange Crêpes.

Orangeade.

▶ **4 medium oranges**
1 tablespoon Grand Marnier
CREPES
¾ cup plain flour
3 eggs
2 tablespoons oil
¾ cup milk

Spread crêpes with marmalade, fold into quarters. Combine butter, sugar, orange rind and juice in large frying pan, stir over heat until boiling. Cut oranges into segments. Add segments, liqueur and crêpes to pan; cook until crêpes are just hot.

Crêpes: Blend or process flour, eggs, oil and milk until smooth. Heat small crêpe pan, grease well. From jug, pour 2 to 3 tablespoons of batter into pan, swirling batter evenly around. Cook until lightly browned, turn crêpe, lightly brown other side. Repeat with remaining batter.

Serves 4.

ORANGEADE

Citric acid is available from supermarkets and health food stores. Recipe unsuitable to freeze or microwave.

1 cup sugar
3 cups water
1 cinnamon stick
2 teaspoons grated orange rind
4 cups (1 litre) strained fresh orange juice
2 teaspoons citric acid

Combine sugar, water and cinnamon

Spatchcocks with Orange Sauce.

stick in large saucepan, stir constantly over heat, without boiling, until sugar is dissolved. Remove from heat, add orange rind, cool to room temperature. Strain sugar syrup into bowl through fine cloth. Stir orange juice and citric acid into syrup, refrigerate until cold.

Makes about 8 cups.

SPATCHCOCKS WITH ORANGE SAUCE

Grand Marnier is an orange-flavoured liqueur. This recipe is unsuitable to freeze or microwave.

3 x No 5 spatchcocks
60g butter, melted
1 clove garlic, crushed
1 tablespoon oil
30g butter, extra
2 medium onions, sliced
2 tablespoons Grand Marnier
¼ cup dry white wine
2 cups orange juice
45g packet French onion soup
¼ cup finely shredded orange rind
½ teaspoon dried tarragon leaves

Cut spatchcocks in half, place cut side down in a single layer in baking dish, brush with combined butter and garlic. Bake in moderate oven 30 minutes or until golden brown.

Heat oil and extra butter in frying pan, add onions, cook, stirring, until onions are soft; add liqueur, wine and 1 cup of the orange juice. Bring to boil, reduce heat, simmer, uncovered, until reduced by half, add remaining orange juice, dry soup mix, orange rind and tarragon, simmer 1 minute. Pour sauce over spatchcocks, cover, bake in moderate oven 15 minutes.

Serves 6.

PASSIONFRUIT

Passionfruit originally came from South and Central America, and the West Indies; it was introduced to Britain in the early 1800s and later to Australia.

PASSIONFRUIT SKIN JAM

This jam will keep for a year; store in refrigerator. Recipe unsuitable to freeze or microwave.

12 large passionfruit
6 cups (1½ litres) water
⅓ cup lemon juice
sugar

Remove pulp from passionfruit and reserve, this is added to jam later. Place skins in large saucepan, add water and lemon juice, cover, bring to boil, reduce heat, simmer, covered, 20 to 30 minutes or until pulpy remains inside skins puff up and become soft enough to remove from outer layer.

Test a few skins before removing them all from the heat. The inside pulpy part should be a burgundy colour, and should scrape away easily with a teaspoon. Drain, reserve liquid.

Scrape all skins until they are free from pulp, discard outer skins. Measure pulp, allow 1 cup sugar to each cup of pulp. Place pulp and sugar in large saucepan with reserved liquid; mixture should not be more than 5cm deep at this stage.

Stir constantly over heat, without boiling, until sugar is dissolved, bring to boil, boil rapidly, without stirring, until mixture will set when tested on a cold saucer; this will take about 40 minutes. Add reserved passionfruit pulp, stand 10 minutes before pouring into hot sterilised jars, seal when cold;

Passionfruit Skin Jam.

store in cool dark place.

Makes about 2½ cups.

PASSIONFRUIT MOUSSE MACAROON CAKE

Cake can be made up to a day ahead. Recipe unsuitable to freeze.

200g packet coconut macaroons
1 cup coconut
125g butter, melted
PASSIONFRUIT FILLING
4 eggs, separated
¾ cup castor sugar
250g carton light sour cream
1 tablespoon gelatine
¼ cup water
¾ cup passionfruit pulp

Crush macaroons in blender or processor, combine in bowl with coconut and butter. Press coconut mixture evenly over base and side of 20cm springform tin, freeze for about 30 minutes while making filling.

Pour filling into coconut crust. Refrigerate several hours or until set.

Passionfruit Filling: Beat egg yolks and sugar in small bowl with electric mixer until thick and creamy, stir in sour cream. Add gelatine to water, dissolve over hot water (or microwave on HIGH for 20 seconds), cool to warm. Stir gelatine mixture into egg yolk mixture, refrigerate until partly set, stir in passionfruit pulp. Fold in firmly beaten egg whites.

PASSIONFRUIT ISLANDS WITH BANANA MANGO CREAM

This recipe is unsuitable to freeze or microwave.

3 egg whites
½ cup castor sugar
½ cup passionfruit pulp
1 small over-ripe banana
1 small mango
¾ cup milk
2 egg yolks
¼ cup castor sugar, extra
TOFFEE
¼ cup sugar
¼ cup corn syrup

Beat egg whites in small bowl with electric mixer until soft peaks form, gradually add sugar, beat until dissolved; gently fold in passionfruit pulp.

Bring large frying pan of water to boil, reduce heat until water is simmering. Mould passionfruit mixture into egg shapes using two dessertspoons. Drop shapes into simmering water, poach on one side for about a minute, gently turn with slotted spoon, poach another minute. Remove the "islands" from water with slotted spoon, drain on absorbent paper; cool. Continue poaching with remaining mixture.

Mash banana with fork; you need 2 tablespoons banana. Purée flesh of mango; you need ½ cup purée.

Bring milk to the boil in saucepan, remove from heat. Beat egg yolks and extra sugar in small bowl with electric mixer until thick and creamy. Gradually stir egg yolk mixture into hot milk, stir constantly over heat, without boiling, until mixture thickens slightly. Remove from heat, stir in banana and mango. Pour into serving dish, top with islands, decorate with toffee.

Toffee: Stir sugar and corn syrup in saucepan over heat, without boiling, until sugar dissolves. Boil rapidly, uncovered, without stirring, until mixture turns a light golden brown; remove from heat, allow bubbles to subside. Dip two teaspoons back to back into toffee and pull toffee into thin strands.

Serves 6.

ABOVE: Passionfruit Mousse Macaroon Cake.
BELOW: Passionfruit Islands with Banana Mango Cream.

PEACHES

Peaches originated in China, where they have been cultivated for thousands of years. There are two types of peaches available: free stone and cling stone. To remove the skin, drop peaches into a saucepan of boiling water, return to the boil, drain, place into bowl of iced water, then peel skin.

Peach Relish.

PEACH RELISH

Relish can be stored in the refrigerator for up to 3 months. Recipe not suitable to freeze or microwave.

2 tablespoons oil
2 cloves garlic, crushed
1 small fresh red chilli, finely chopped
1 tablespoon yellow mustard seeds
2 medium onions, chopped
2 medium red peppers, chopped
2 medium green peppers, chopped
2kg peaches, chopped
2 cups white vinegar
1 cup brown sugar, lightly packed

Heat oil in large saucepan or boiler, add garlic, chilli, mustard seeds and onions, cook 1 minute.

Add peppers, cook further 1 minute. Add peaches, vinegar and brown sugar, stir constantly over heat, without boiling, until sugar is dissolved. Bring to boil, reduce heat, simmer, uncovered, without stirring, 45 minutes or until relish is thick.

Relish will need to be stirred occasionally towards the end of cooking time to prevent sticking. Pour into hot sterilised jars, seal when cold.

Makes about 5 cups.

ALMOND PEACH FLANS

Kirsch is a cherry-flavoured liqueur. This recipe is unsuitable to freeze or microwave.

ALMOND PASTRY
1¼ cups plain flour
2 tablespoons icing sugar
125g butter, chopped
2 tablespoons packaged ground almonds
2 egg yolks
1 teaspoon water, approximately
6 medium peaches
½ cup apricot jam
2 teaspoons Kirsch
CREAMY CUSTARD FILLING
8 egg yolks

1 cup castor sugar
2 tablespoons cornflour
2 cups milk
2 teaspoons vanilla essence
2 tablespoons Kirsch

Almond Pastry: Sift flour and icing sugar into bowl, rub in butter. Stir in almonds, then egg yolks and enough water to make ingredients cling together. Knead gently on lightly floured surface until smooth. Cover, refrigerate 30 minutes.

Divide pastry into 6 equal portions.

Almond Peach Flans.

Roll each piece between 2 sheets plastic wrap. Line 6 x 10cm flan tins (with removable bases) with pastry, trim edges. Prick pastry all over with a fork, bake in moderately hot oven for about 15 minutes or until golden brown. Cool 5 minutes, remove cases from tins.

Peel and stone peaches. Cut half the peaches into slices. Chop remaining peaches finely. Stir finely chopped peaches into filling. Divide peach mixture between pastry cases, arrange sliced peaches on top of flans.

Heat combined apricot jam and liqueur in small saucepan, strain. Spoon apricot glaze over flans, refrigerate 15 minutes or until glaze is set.

Creamy Custard Filling: Whisk egg yolks, sugar and cornflour together in bowl until thick. Heat milk in saucepan, gradually stir in egg yolk mixture, stir constantly over heat until mixture boils and thickens. Stir in essence and liqueur; cover to prevent skin forming, cool, refrigerate until cold.

Makes 6.

PEACHY PORK ROAST

This recipe is unsuitable to freeze or microwave.

1½kg loin pork, boned
2 tablespoons oil
SPICY SEASONING
1 medium peach, chopped
¾ cup stale breadcrumbs
1 medium onion, finely chopped
1 teaspoon canned green
 peppercorns, crushed
2 tablespoons chutney

►

PEACHES

▶ PEACH SAUCE

4 medium peaches, chopped
1 medium onion, chopped
2 teaspoons grated fresh ginger
½ cup water
2 teaspoons light soya sauce
2 tablespoons sugar, approximately

Spread seasoning over pork flap, roll pork tightly, tie with string at 5cm intervals. Brush pork with oil, place in baking dish. Bake in hot oven 30 minutes, reduce heat to moderate, bake further 1 hour or until tender, turning pork once. Serve hot or cold with sauce.

Spicy Seasoning: Combine peach, breadcrumbs, onion, peppercorns and chutney in bowl; mix well.

Peach Sauce: Place peaches in saucepan with onion, ginger, water and soya sauce. Bring to boil, reduce heat, simmer, covered, 15 minutes or until peaches are pulpy and onion soft. Blend or process until smooth. Add sugar to taste; amount will depend on ripeness of peaches.

Serves 6.

Peachy Pork Roast.

PEARS

Pears are members of the rose family. The European pear has been cultivated in Europe since ancient times. A list exists which shows that 232 varieties were known in the 16th century. The main varieties grown in Australia are Williams, Bartlett and Packham. They can be eaten with or without skin.

China: Villeroy & Boch

Nutty Pears with Rich Caramel Sauce.

Pear and Ginger Custard Dessert.

NUTTY PEARS WITH RICH CARAMEL SAUCE

This recipe is not suitable to freeze or microwave.

15g butter
1 tablespoon honey
¼ cup chopped pecans or walnuts
¼ cup muesli
¼ cup coconut
6 medium pears
RICH CARAMEL SAUCE
90g butter
¾ cup brown sugar, lightly packed
300ml carton cream
3 teaspoons cornflour
1 tablespoon water

Combine butter and honey in small saucepan, stir over heat until butter is melted, stir in nuts, muesli and coconut. Peel pears, remove cores, leaving hollow centres. Fill centres with nut mixture. Place pears into ovenproof dish, top with sauce, cover, bake in moderate oven for about 1 hour or until pears are tender. Serve with sauce.

Rich Caramel Sauce: Melt butter in saucepan, stir in sugar, stir constantly over heat, without boiling, until sugar is dissolved. Stir in cream and blended cornflour and water, stir constantly over heat until mixture boils and thickens. Serve hot or cold.

Serves 6.

PEAR AND GINGER CUSTARD DESSERT

This recipe is not suitable to freeze or microwave.

185g butter
⅔ cup castor sugar
3 eggs
¼ cup packaged ground almonds
1¼ cups self-raising flour
½ cup milk
2 large pears, thickly sliced
¼ cup slivered almonds

GINGER CUSTARD
2 tablespoons custard powder
2 tablespoons sugar
2 teaspoons ground ginger
1⅓ cups milk
30g butter

Cream butter and sugar in small bowl with electric mixer until light and fluffy. Beat in eggs one at a time, beat until combined. Transfer mixture to large bowl, stir in ground almonds, half the sifted flour and half the milk, then stir in remaining flour and milk.

Spread custard into greased ovenproof dish (2 litres (8 cups) capacity) top with pears in single layer. Spread pears with cake mixture, sprinkle with slivered almonds. Bake in moderate oven for about 1¼ hours.

Ginger Custard: Combine custard powder, sugar and ginger in saucepan, gradually stir in milk. Stir constantly over heat until mixture boils and thickens. Stir in butter.

►

PEARS

▶ **PEAR AND BLUE CHEESE SALAD**

This recipe is not suitable to freeze or microwave.

½ cup slivered almonds
1 cup plain yoghurt
1 tablespoon chopped fresh chives
2 teaspoons sugar
2 tablespoons orange juice
4 medium pears, sliced
175g blue cheese, crumbled
4 sticks celery, chopped
1 lettuce

Toast almonds on oven tray in moderate oven for 5 minutes.

Combine yoghurt, chives, sugar and orange juice in large bowl, add pears, mix gently, stir in cheese and celery. Line bowl with lettuce, add pear mixture, serve sprinkled with almonds.

Serves 4.

Pear and Blue Cheese Salad.

Bowl: Villeroy & Boch

PEPPERS

Peppers (capsicums) originated in South America, and there are hundreds of varieties in all shapes, sizes and colours, with flavours ranging from mild to hot. The ones most commonly used are the red and green bell peppers.

ITALIAN DRIED PEPPERS

Peppers can be stored in refrigerator for up to 6 months. Recipe unsuitable to freeze or microwave.

2kg peppers, quartered
4 cloves garlic, peeled
2 teaspoons dried rosemary leaves
2 teaspoons dried tarragon leaves
olive oil

Place peppers cut side down on wire rack, bake in very slow oven for about 4 hours or until peppers are dry. Turn and rearrange peppers during drying process. Pack peppers into hot sterilised jars with garlic and herbs, pour enough oil over peppers to cover completely; seal jars.

Italian Dried Peppers.

Peppers with Olive Sambal.

PEPPERS WITH OLIVE SAMBAL

Serve as an accompaniment to curry, or cold or barbecued meat. Recipe unsuitable to freeze or microwave.

3 medium red peppers
3 medium green peppers
3 medium yellow peppers
½ teaspoon dried oregano leaves
¼ cup olive oil
¼ teaspoon ground black pepper
oil for deep-frying
BATTER
¾ cup plain flour
¼ teaspoon bicarbonate of soda
1 cup iced water
1 egg, lightly beaten
1 tablespoon oil
OLIVE SAMBAL
¼ cup pitted chopped black olives
¼ cup chopped pimiento-stuffed olives
½ teaspoon dried oregano leaves
1 clove garlic, crushed
¼ cup olive oil
1 small fresh red chilli, chopped

Cut peppers in half lengthways, remove seeds. Place half the peppers, cut side down, on oven tray. Bake in moderate oven 20 minutes, cool slightly. Peel peppers, cut peppers into 2cm strips. Combine peppers, oregano, oil and black pepper in bowl. Place peppers on oven tray in single layer, bake in moderate oven 3 minutes or until heated through.

Cut remaining peppers into 2cm strips. Dip into batter, deep-fry in hot oil a few at a time until crisp; drain on absorbent paper. Serve with sambal.

Batter: Blend or process all ingredients until smooth.

Olive Sambal: Combine all ingredients in small bowl.

Serves 6 to 8.

►

PEPPERS

▶ GREEN PEPPER TERRINE

Terrine can be made up to a day ahead.
Recipe unsuitable to freeze.

½ bunch English spinach
2 medium green peppers
2 bacon rashers, finely chopped
250g packet cream cheese
250g ricotta cheese
2 tablespoons chopped fresh chives
2 tablespoons corn relish
pinch cayenne pepper

Lightly oil 8cm x 26cm bar pan, line with plastic wrap.

Boil, steam or microwave spinach until wilted, rinse under cold water, pat dry with absorbent paper. Line base and sides of pan with spinach leaves, overlapping sides.

Cut peppers into quarters, remove seeds, place on oven tray, cut side down, grill until skins blister. Peel off skins. Cook bacon in a small frying pan until crisp.

Beat cheeses in medium bowl with electric mixer until smooth; add bacon, chives, relish and cayenne pepper. Spread one-third of the cheese mixture into prepared pan, top with half the peppers. Repeat layering with remaining mixture, finishing with a cheese layer. Fold spinach over the loaf, refrigerate 2 hours or overnight.

Green Pepper Terrine.

PINEAPPLES

Pineapples are native to South America, Mexico and the West Indies; it is believed they originated in Brazil and Paraguay.

PINEAPPLE AND PECAN RICE SALAD WITH CURRY DRESSING

This recipe is unsuitable to freeze or microwave.

1 cup brown rice
½ medium pineapple, chopped
4 green shallots, chopped
1 small apple, chopped
1 cup chopped pecans
2 tablespoons chopped raisins
CURRY DRESSING
¼ cup oil
¼ cup white vinegar
1 tablespoon curry powder
1½ tablespoons sugar

Add rice gradually to large saucepan of boiling water, boil rapidly, uncovered, for about 30 minutes or until just tender, drain; rinse under cold water; drain.

Combine rice and pineapple with

ABOVE: Chicken and Pineapple Stir-Fry. BELOW: Pineapple and Pecan Rice Salad with Curry Dressing.

remaining ingredients in large bowl; mix in dressing just before serving.
Curry Dressing: Combine all ingredients in jar; shake well.

Serves 4.

CHICKEN AND PINEAPPLE STIR-FRY

This recipe is unsuitable to freeze or microwave.

1 tablespoon oil
1 teaspoon grated fresh ginger
1 clove garlic, crushed
1 medium onion, chopped
1 medium red pepper, sliced
1 small bunch asparagus, chopped
1 small pineapple, chopped
1 tablespoon oil, extra
1 tablespoon oyster sauce
1 tablespoon light soya sauce
1 teaspoon hot chilli sauce
500g chicken thigh fillets, sliced
2 teaspoons cornflour
2 tablespoons water

Heat oil in wok or frying pan, add ginger, garlic and onion, stir-fry 1 minute. Add pepper, asparagus and pineapple, stir-fry 1 minute, remove from pan.

Heat extra oil in pan, add sauces ▶

China: Limoges; tiles: Country Floors

Dish: John Dermer, Pottery, Yackandandah, Vic; background: House of Bambuzit

PINEAPPLES

Pineapple with Fruit Mince and Brandy Sauce.

▶ then quarter of the chicken; stir-fry few minutes or until chicken is tender, remove from pan. Continue to fry remaining chicken in the same way.

Blend cornflour with water, add to pan with vegetables and chicken, stir-fry until mixture boils and thickens.

Serves 4.

PINEAPPLE WITH FRUIT MINCE AND BRANDY SAUCE

Fruit mince can be prepared up to a month ahead. Recipe unsuitable to freeze or microwave.

1 medium pineapple, sliced
30g butter
2 teaspoons brown sugar

FRUIT MINCE
¼ cup chopped raisins
¼ cup chopped dried apricots
2 tablespoons chopped glacé cherries
¼ cup currants
2 tablespoons pine nuts
2 tablespoons brown sugar
2 tablespoons brandy
¼ teaspoon ground cinnamon
1 teaspoon grated lemon rind

BRANDY SAUCE
3 teaspoons cornflour
2 tablespoons sugar
½ cup milk
½ cup cream
1 teaspoon butter
2 tablespoons brandy

Remove core from pineapple slices, place slices on oven tray in single layer. Melt butter in saucepan, stir in sugar, brush over pineapple; grill for about 5 minutes or until glazed. Place pineapple on serving plates, fill centres of each slice with fruit mince, top slices with sauce.

Fruit Mince: Combine fruit, pine nuts, sugar, brandy, cinnamon and lemon rind; mix well, cover, stand overnight.

Brandy Sauce: Blend cornflour and sugar with milk in saucepan, stir in cream and butter, stir the sauce constantly over heat until mixture boils and thickens; remove from heat, stir in brandy.

Serves 4 to 6.

PLUMS

Plums have grown wild in the northern hemisphere from the Pacific coast in America to Japan. To peel: use a sharp knife or vegetable peeler.

Plum Swirl Cheesecake.

PLUM SWIRL CHEESECAKE

Recipe can be made a day ahead; it is unsuitable to freeze or microwave.

CRUMB CRUST
125g butter, melted
2 cups plain sweet biscuit crumbs
CREAMY PLUM FILLING
500g yellow plums, chopped
1 tablespoon water
2 tablespoons lemon juice
125g packet cream cheese
½ cup castor sugar
3 eggs
300ml carton thickened cream

Crumb Crust: Combine butter and crumbs in bowl, mix well, press evenly over base and side of 23cm flan tin. Refrigerate 30 minutes.

Pour plum mixture into crumb crust, pour in cheese mixture; swirl through with knife for marbled effect. Bake in moderately slow oven for about 1 hour or until set. Cool in oven with door ajar; refrigerate before serving.

Creamy Plum Filling: Combine plums, water and half the lemon juice in large saucepan, cover, bring to boil, reduce heat, simmer, covered, for about 10 minutes or until plums are soft. Reduce heat, simmer, stirring constantly, for about 10 minutes or until mixture is thick; allow mixture to cool to room temperature.

Combine cheese, sugar and remaining lemon juice in small bowl,

beat with electric mixer until smooth. Beat in eggs one at a time, beating well after each addition. Add cream, beat until combined.

PLUM ICE-CREAM

Recipe unsuitable to microwave.

750g red plums, chopped
½ cup lemon juice
½ cup water
¾ cup castor sugar
6 egg yolks
½ cup castor sugar, extra
300ml carton thickened cream
1 teaspoon vanilla essence
300ml carton thickened cream, extra

Combine plums, lemon juice and water in large saucepan, bring to boil, reduce heat, simmer, covered, for about 15 minutes or until plums are tender. Add sugar, stir over heat, without boiling, until sugar is dissolved. Bring to boil, reduce heat, simmer, uncovered, with- ▶

PLUMS

Plum Ice-Cream.

▶ out stirring, for 15 minutes; strain, cool. Refrigerate several hours.

Whisk egg yolks and extra sugar in large heatproof bowl over simmering water until sugar is dissolved. Gradually whisk in cream, whisk constantly over simmering water until mixture is slightly thickened, stir in essence. Pour custard into bowl, cover, cool, refrigerate custard 1 hour.

Fold cold plum mixture through custard, then fold in extra whipped cream. Pour into deep 23cm square cake pan, cover with foil, freeze several hours or until firm. Remove from freezer, spoon mixture into medium bowl, beat with electric mixer until smooth. Return mixture to cake pan, cover; freeze ice-cream several hours or until firm.

Makes about 2 litres.

CHICKEN WITH FRESH PLUM SAUCE

This recipe is unsuitable to freeze or microwave.

8 chicken breast fillets
⅓ cup cornflour
1 teaspoon five spice powder
125g butter
2 large onions, sliced
2 sticks celery, sliced
1 medium green pepper, sliced
PLUM SAUCE
1 tablespoon oil
1 large onion, chopped
2 cloves garlic, crushed
2 teaspoons grated fresh ginger
750g red plums, chopped
¼ cup brown sugar
¼ cup water
2 teaspoons light soya sauce

Cut chicken into thin strips, toss in combined cornflour and five spice powder. Melt butter in frying pan or wok, add chicken in batches, stir-fry until lightly browned and tender; remove from pan. Add onions, celery and pepper to pan (add a little extra butter, if necessary); stir-fry until vegetables are tender. Add plum sauce, stir-fry until heated through.

Plum Sauce: Heat oil in frying pan or wok, add onion, garlic and ginger, stir-fry until onion is soft. Add plums, sugar, water and soya sauce, cover, bring to boil, reduce heat, simmer, uncovered, until mixture is pulpy.

Serves 6.

Chicken with Fresh Plum Sauce.

Bowl: Mid-City House & Garden

PUMPKINS

Pumpkins are members of the gourd family, and are among the oldest edible plants cultivated by man. They originated in northern Argentina, Mexico and Central America. The most common pumpkins in Australia are the Queensland blue, butternut and banana.

GOLDEN RAISIN 'N' NUT DAMPER

Damper is best served hot with butter. It can be frozen for up to 1 month. To reheat, wrap in foil while frozen, bake in moderate oven for about 30 minutes. You will need to boil, steam or microwave about 375g pumpkin. Damper unsuitable to microwave.

1 cup mashed pumpkin
1 egg, lightly beaten
¼ cup milk
2½ cups self-raising flour
¼ teaspoon ground cinnamon
60g butter
¼ cup castor sugar
¼ cup chopped pecans or walnuts
¼ cup chopped raisins
1 tablespoon milk, extra
1 tablespoon castor sugar, extra

▶

PUMPKINS

Golden Raisin 'N' Nut Damper.

▶ Sieve pumpkin into bowl, stir in egg and milk. Sift flour and cinnamon into bowl, rub in butter. Stir in sugar, nuts and raisins then pumpkin mixture. Knead on floured surface until smooth.

Place dough onto greased oven tray, press out with fingers to a circle about 2cm thick. Brush with extra milk, sprinkle with extra sugar. Mark into 8 wedges. Bake in moderately hot oven for about 30 minutes or until golden brown and damper sounds hollow when tapped lightly with fingers.

PUMPKIN LIQUEUR CHEESECAKE

You will need to boil, steam or microwave about 750g pumpkin for this recipe. We used butternut pumpkin for its delicate flavour; do not add butter or milk when mashing pumpkin. Grand Marnier is an orange-flavoured liqueur. This recipe is unsuitable to freeze or microwave.

1 cup plain sweet biscuit crumbs
60g butter, melted

ORANGE CREAM CHEESE FILLING
2 x 250g packets cream cheese
¾ cup brown sugar, firmly packed
5 eggs
2 cups cold mashed pumpkin
¼ cup Grand Marnier
2 tablespoons grated orange rind
¼ cup orange juice
SOUR CREAM TOPPING
300g carton sour cream
¼ cup Grand Marnier
¼ cup castor sugar
Combine biscuits and butter. Press

100

ABOVE: Pumpkin Liqueur Cheesecake. RIGHT: Pumpkin, Bacon and Chive Ring.

over base of 23cm springform tin; refrigerate 30 minutes. Pour filling into tin, bake in moderate oven 50 minutes or until set around edge. Remove from oven, quickly spread with topping, bake further 10 minutes. Cool, refrigerate overnight.

Orange Cream Cheese Filling: Beat cream cheese and sugar in medium bowl with electric mixer until smooth. Beat in eggs one at a time, beat in pumpkin, liqueur, rind and juice.

Sour Cream Topping: Combine all ingredients in bowl, mix well.

PUMPKIN, BACON AND CHIVE RING

Cook pumpkin ring as close to serving time as possible. You will need to boil, steam or microwave about 1kg pumpkin for this recipe. Ring is unsuitable to freeze or microwave.

3 cups mashed pumpkin
⅔ cup thickened cream
⅓ cup stale breadcrumbs
4 eggs
2 bacon rashers, finely chopped
1 medium onion, finely chopped
1 clove garlic, crushed
1 cup grated tasty cheese
2 tablespoons chopped fresh chives
60g butter
2 medium onions, sliced, extra
2 tablespoons chopped fresh parsley
1 cup stale breadcrumbs, extra

Process pumpkin until smooth. Add cream, breadcrumbs and eggs, process until combined. Pour pumpkin mixture into bowl.

Heat frying pan, add bacon, onion and garlic, cook until onion is soft. Add onion mixture to pumpkin mixture with cheese and chives. Pour into greased 24cm savarin or 20cm ring pan.

Place pan in baking dish with enough hot water to come halfway up side of pan. Bake in moderate oven 50 minutes. Remove from baking dish, stand 10 minutes before turning out.

Heat half the butter in frying pan, add extra onions, cook, stirring, until lightly browned, stir in parsley. Sprinkle over ring. Heat remaining butter in pan, add extra breadcrumbs, stir until golden brown, sprinkle over ring.

RASPBERRIES

Raspberries have been eaten in Europe since prehistoric times. In England, raspberry cultivation dates from the 17th century.

RASPBERRY AND WHITE CHOCOLATE MOUSSE

Mousse can be prepared up to 2 days ahead. Framboise is a raspberry-flavoured liqueur. This recipe is unsuitable to freeze.

400g fresh raspberries
200g white chocolate, chopped
1 tablespoon gelatine
¼ cup water
3 egg yolks
300ml carton thickened cream
¼ cup icing sugar
2 tablespoons Framboise

Blend or process raspberries until smooth; strain to remove seeds.

Melt chocolate over hot water, cool; do not allow to set.

Sprinkle gelatine over water, dissolve over hot water (or microwave on HIGH for about 30 seconds). Pour

Raspberry and White Chocolate Mousse.

Napkin: Australian East India Co.; tiles: Country Floors

Plate: Hampshire & Lowndes; spoon: Mikasa; accessories: Australian East India Co.

Waffles with Fresh Raspberry Sauce.

gelatine mixture into large bowl, cool slightly, do not allow to set.

Add egg yolks and chocolate to gelatine mixture, whisk until pale and glossy. Whip cream and sifted icing sugar together until soft peaks form. Fold into chocolate mixture with raspberry purée and liqueur. Pour into lightly wetted mould (5 cup capacity). Refrigerate several hours or overnight.

Serves 4 to 6.

WAFFLES WITH FRESH RASPBERRY SAUCE

Recipe can be frozen for 2 months; it is unsuitable to microwave.

WAFFLES
1¾ cups plain flour
¼ cup self-raising flour
¼ cup castor sugar
2 eggs, separated
1½ cups milk
60g butter, melted
2 tablespoons cold water
RASPBERRY SAUCE
½ cup sugar
½ cup water
500g fresh raspberries
Waffles: Sift flours and sugar into large bowl, make well in centre, gradually stir in combined egg yolks and milk, then butter and water; stir until smooth.

Fold in softly beaten egg whites.

Drop about 2 tablespoons mixture onto prepared waffle iron. Close iron, cook for about 2 minutes or until golden brown. Serve waffles with ice-cream and sauce.

Raspberry Sauce: Combine sugar and water in small saucepan, stir constantly over heat, without boiling, until sugar is dissolved. Bring to boil, boil rapidly, without stirring, for 3 minutes; cool 10 minutes. Blend or process half the raspberries with the sugar syrup; transfer to bowl, stir in remaining raspberries, refrigerate before serving.

Makes about 10.

◀

RASPBERRIES

▶ FRESH RASPBERRY JAM WITH KIRSCH

Kirsch is a cherry-flavoured liqueur. Recipe unsuitable to freeze.

3 cups water
4 cups sugar
1kg fresh raspberries
1 teaspoon grated lemon rind
2 tablespoons Kirsch

Combine water, sugar, raspberries and rind in large saucepan or boiler, stir constantly over heat, without boiling, until sugar is dissolved (mixture should not be more than 5cm deep). Bring to boil, boil rapidly, uncovered, without stirring, for about 15 minutes (or microwave on HIGH for about 55 minutes) or until jam will jell when tested on a cold saucer. Stir occasionally towards end of cooking time. Stir in Kirsch, stand 5 minutes, pour into hot sterilised jars, seal when cold.

Makes about 4 cups.

Ceramic pot: Australian East India Co.: tiles: Country Floors

Fresh Raspberry Jam with Kirsch.

RHUBARB

Rhubarb is native to Siberia, the Himalayas and East Asia. There are records of some types of rhubarb as far back as 2000BC. It was used mostly for medicinal purposes. To prepare: cut thick ends from stalks before cooking; never eat the leaves, which are poisonous.

Rhubarb and Apple Jam.

Rhubarb and Apple Sponge Pudding.

RHUBARB AND APPLE JAM

Jam will keep for up to a year in a cool dry place or in refrigerator. Recipe unsuitable to freeze.

8 cups (680g) chopped rhubarb
2 large apples, chopped
1 cup water
2¼ cups sugar, approximately
2 tablespoons lemon juice
Combine rhubarb, apples and water in large saucepan or boiler, cover, bring to boil, reduce heat, simmer 15 minutes (or microwave in shallow dish, covered, on HIGH for about 10 minutes) or until fruit is pulpy.

Measure mixture; allow ¾ cup sugar to each cup of mixture. Return rhubarb mixture, sugar and lemon juice to pan. Stir constantly over heat, without boiling, until sugar is dissolved (mixture should not be more than 5cm deep). Bring to boil, boil as rapidly as possible, uncovered, without stirring, for about 40 minutes (or microwave on HIGH for about 30 minutes), stirring occasionally or until mixture is thick and pulpy when tested on a cold saucer. Tint with a little red food colouring, if desired. Pour mixture into hot sterilised jars; seal when cold.

Makes about 4 cups.

RHUBARB AND APPLE SPONGE PUDDING

This recipe is unsuitable to freeze or microwave.

5 cups (425g) chopped rhubarb
2 medium apples, thinly sliced
½ cup castor sugar
1 teaspoon grated lemon rind
¼ cup water
2 eggs
⅓ cup castor sugar, extra
2 tablespoons cornflour
2 tablespoons plain flour
2 tablespoons self-raising flour
Combine rhubarb, apples, sugar, rind ▶

RHUBARB

Rhubarb Ice-Cream Cake

and water in saucepan, bring to boil, reduce heat, simmer, covered, for about 15 minutes or until tender. Pour hot rhubarb mixture into deep greased ovenproof dish (6 cup capacity).

Beat eggs in small bowl with electric mixer until thick and creamy, gradually add extra sugar, beat until dissolved between each addition. Sift flours over egg mixture, fold through gently. Spread mixture evenly over hot rhubarb mixture, bake in moderate oven for about 30 minutes.

Serves 4 to 6.

RHUBARB ICE-CREAM CAKE

Recipe unsuitable to microwave.
ALMOND CAKE
½ cup blanched almonds
2 tablespoons castor sugar
3 eggs, separated
2 teaspoons vanilla essence
½ cup castor sugar, extra
¼ cup self-raising flour
2 tablespoons plain flour
60g butter, melted
RHUBARB ICE-CREAM
3 cups (255g) chopped rhubarb

½ cup castor sugar
¼ cup water
2 tablespoons lemon juice
red food colouring
1 litre vanilla ice-cream
RHUBARB SAUCE
2 cups (170g) chopped rhubarb
⅓ cup castor sugar
½ cup water
6 passionfruit
2 tablespoons lemon juice

Almond Cake: Toast almonds on oven tray in moderate oven 5 minutes; cool. Blend or process almonds and sugar until finely ground. Beat egg yolks, essence and half the extra sugar together in small bowl with electric mixer until thick and creamy; transfer to large bowl. Stir in almond mixture, sifted flours and butter.

Beat egg whites in small bowl with electric mixer until soft peaks form, add remaining sugar gradually, beat until dissolved, fold into almond mixture in 2 batches.

Pour into greased and base-lined 20cm springform tin, bake in moderate oven 25 minutes. Stand 5 minutes before turning onto wire rack to cool.

Cover base of springform tin with foil, split cake in half, place one half in tin, top with half the rhubarb ice-cream, then remaining cake and ice-cream. Cover, freeze overnight. Serve with sauce.

Rhubarb Ice-Cream: Combine rhubarb, sugar and water in saucepan, stir constantly over heat until sugar is dissolved, bring to boil, reduce heat, simmer, covered, 15 minutes, cool.

Blend or process rhubarb mixture, lemon juice and a little colouring until smooth. Stand ice-cream at room temperature 15 minutes to soften (or microwave on HIGH for about 30 seconds). Beat ice-cream in large bowl with electric mixer until smooth, add rhubarb mixture, beat until combined.

Rhubarb Sauce: Combine rhubarb, sugar and water in saucepan, stir constantly over heat until sugar is dissolved, bring to boil, reduce heat, simmer, covered, 10 minutes; cool.

Push passionfruit pulp through strainer to extract juice (you will need 2 tablespoons). Blend or process passionfruit juice, lemon juice and rhubarb mixture until smooth.

SHALLOTS

Shallots (golden) are gourmet members of the onion family. Grown in France for centuries, shallots are synonymous with French cookery and are an essential ingredient in many recipes. Shallots are used extensively in restaurants.

GOLDEN SHALLOT TARTLETS

This recipe is unsuitable to freeze or microwave.

PASTRY
1½ cups plain flour
125g butter
2 egg yolks, lightly beaten
1 tablespoon water, approximately
1 egg white, lightly beaten
TANGY SHALLOT FILLING
60g butter
250g golden shallots, finely chopped
3 eggs, lightly beaten
300ml carton cream
30g blue cheese

Pastry: Sift flour into bowl, rub in butter. Add egg yolks and enough water to make ingredients cling together. Press dough into a ball, cover, refrigerate 30 minutes.

Roll pastry to line 6 x 11cm flan tins. Place tins on oven tray. Prick pastry all over with fork, bake in moderately hot oven for about 15 minutes or until golden brown. Brush sides and bases with egg white; cool. Pour filling into cases, bake in moderate oven for about 15 minutes or until filling is set.

Tangy Shallot Filling: Heat butter in frying pan, add shallots, cook, stirring constantly, until shallots are soft, drain on absorbent paper; cool.

Combine eggs, cream, crumbled cheese and shallots in medium bowl; mix with a fork until combined.

Makes 6. ▶

China: Villeroy & Boch

Golden Shallot Tartlets

SHALLOTS

Dish: Villeroy & Boch; table: Keyhole Furniture

LEFT:
Caramelised
Golden
Shallots.
BELOW:
Golden
Shallot
Salad.

► **CARAMELISED GOLDEN SHALLOTS**

Serve as an accompaniment vegetable. This recipe is unsuitable to freeze or microwave.

500g golden shallots
90g butter
¼ cup water
¼ cup brown sugar
Peel shallots, trim bases slightly. Melt butter in saucepan, add shallots, cook over very low heat for about 20 minutes or until shallots are tender and golden brown; stir occasionally (do not allow butter to burn). Stir in water and sugar, stir over low heat until sauce is thick and syrupy.
Serves 4.

GOLDEN SHALLOT SALAD

This recipe is unsuitable to freeze or microwave.

500g golden shallots
¼ cup castor sugar
2 cups white vinegar
1 tablespoon sesame seeds
1 lettuce
2 x 250g punnets cherry tomatoes, halved
60g mozzarella cheese, chopped
BASIL DRESSING
⅔ cup olive oil
1 tablespoon chopped fresh basil

Platter, salt & pepper shakers: Villeroy & Boch; table: Keyhole Furniture

Break shallots into segments, place in jar. Combine sugar and vinegar in saucepan, stir constantly over heat until sugar is dissolved. Bring to the boil, pour over shallots; seal while hot. Stand at least overnight before using.

Toast sesame seeds on oven tray in moderate oven for 5 minutes.

Remove shallots from jar, reserve ¼ cup vinegar for the dressing; slice shallots. Arrange lettuce on serving plate, add shallots, tomatoes, cheese, dressing and sesame seeds.
Basil Dressing: Combine ingredients in jar; shake well.
Serves 4.

108

SNOW PEAS

There is no evidence of when snow peas were first cultivated. It appears they were developed in later years as an edible pod pea. To prepare: top and tail peas; pull away strings from older, larger peas.

SNOW PEAS WITH PRAWNS AND MANGO

This recipe is not suitable to freeze or microwave.

500g snow peas
1kg cooked king prawns
1 large mango, sliced
ORANGE HOLLANDAISE SAUCE
4 egg yolks
2 teaspoons grated orange rind
1 tablespoon orange juice
125g butter

Boil, steam or microwave snow peas for about 30 seconds or until bright green. Rinse with cold water, drain. Shell prawns, leaving tails intact; remove back vein. Serve snow peas, prawns and mango with sauce.

Orange Hollandaise Sauce: Combine egg yolks, orange rind and juice in blender, blend until smooth. Gradually add hot bubbling butter while motor is operating. Blend until thick.
Serves 4.

CURRIED CHICKEN WITH SNOW PEAS

Recipe unsuitable to freeze.

30g butter
375g snow peas
1 small red pepper, sliced
30g butter, extra
4 chicken breast fillets
1 large onion, chopped
2 cloves garlic, crushed
2 teaspoons curry powder
½ teaspoon ground cardamom
½ teaspoon ground cumin
200ml carton coconut cream
½ cup water
2 tablespoons peanut butter
1 tablespoon lemon juice

►

Plate: Made Where; fork: The Bay Tree

Snow Peas with Prawns and Mango.

SNOW PEAS

Caption: **Curried Chicken with Snow Peas.**

Plate, jug & cutlery: The Bay Tree; fabric: Les Olivades; table: John Normyle

► Heat butter in frying pan, add snow peas and pepper, stir constantly over heat (or microwave on HIGH for about 5 minutes) until just tender.

Heat extra butter in separate frying pan, add chicken, cook gently (or microwave on HIGH for about 5 min-utes) until chicken is just tender; remove from pan, drain on absorbent paper; cut chicken into slices.

Add onion, garlic, curry, cardamom and cumin to pan, stir constantly over heat (or microwave on HIGH for about 3 minutes) until onion is soft.

Add coconut cream, water, peanut butter and lemon juice, bring to boil, add chicken, stir until heated through (or microwave on HIGH for about 3 minutes). Serve chicken in sauce with peas and pepper.

Serves 4.

SNOW PEA SALAD WITH HOT HONEY DRESSING

Recipe unsuitable to freeze.

500g snow peas
1 cup bean sprouts
250g punnet cherry tomatoes, halved
HOT HONEY DRESSING
⅔ cup water
1 small chicken stock cube, crumbled
⅓ cup honey
2 teaspoons hot chilli sauce
1 teaspoon grated fresh ginger
1 teaspoon cornflour
2 teaspoons water, extra

Boil, steam or microwave snow peas until just tender, drain; rinse under cold water, drain. Combine in bowl with sprouts and tomatoes. Top with hot dressing just before serving.

Hot Honey Dressing: Combine water, stock cube, honey, sauce and ginger in saucepan, stir over heat until combined. Stir in blended cornflour and extra water, stir constantly over heat (or microwave on HIGH for about 3 minutes) until mixture boils and thickens.

Serves 4.

Table - John Normyle

Snow Pea Salad with Hot Honey Dressing.

SPINACH

Spinach (English) originated in Persia and, by the end of the 1500s, was popular in England. Silver beet can be substituted for English spinach in most recipes. To prepare: remove leaves from the stems, discard stems, wash and drain well before cooking. ▶

Spinach Chicken Terrine.

SPINACH

Creamy Spinach Soup.

loaf dish with spinach leaves, reserving a few leaves for top of terrine.

Spread half the chicken filling into dish, top with spinach filling, then spread with remaining chicken filling. Top with remaining spinach leaves, cover with foil. Place terrine in baking dish with enough hot water to come halfway up sides of dish. Bake in moderate oven for about 1 hour or until set. Remove dish from water, stand 5 minutes. Remove foil, invert terrine onto serving dish. Serve warm or cold with sauce.

Chicken Filling: Melt butter in frying pan, add onion, bacon and curry powder, stir constantly over heat until onion is soft. Process onion mixture, chicken, cream and eggs until smooth.

Spinach Filling: Melt butter in saucepan, add garlic and spinach, stir over heat until spinach is soft. Drain, press out as much moisture as possible. Combine spinach, rice, cream, egg and nutmeg in bowl, mix well.

Tomato Sauce: Combine all ingredients in saucepan, bring to boil, reduce heat, simmer, covered, 10 minutes. Blend or process until smooth; strain. Reheat before serving.

CREAMY SPINACH SOUP

Soup can be made up to a day ahead or frozen for up to 3 months.

1 tablespoon oil
1 clove garlic, crushed
3 bunches English spinach
2 cups water
60g butter
2 tablespoons plain flour
1½ cups milk
250g carton sour cream
30g butter, extra
1 medium onion, finely chopped
3 bacon rashers, chopped

Heat oil in large saucepan, add garlic and spinach, cook, stirring, 3 minutes. Cover, cook (or microwave on HIGH for 2 minutes) until tender.

Blend or process spinach with water until smooth.

Melt butter in saucepan, stir in flour, stir over heat 1 minute. Gradually stir in milk and sour cream, stir constantly over heat (or microwave on HIGH for about 3 minutes) until sauce boils and thickens. Add spinach purée, reduce heat, simmer, stirring, 5 minutes (or microwave on HIGH about 2 minutes).

Heat extra butter in saucepan, add onion and bacon, cook, stirring, until onion is soft (or microwave on HIGH for 3 minutes); stir into spinach mixture. Reheat before serving.

Serves 6.

▶ SPINACH CHICKEN TERRINE

You will need to cook ¼ cup of rice for this recipe. The terrine can be made up to 2 days ahead. Tomato sauce can be made up to a day ahead. Recipe unsuitable to freeze or microwave.

1 bunch English spinach
CHICKEN FILLING
15g butter
1 medium onion, finely chopped
2 bacon rashers, chopped
2 teaspoons curry powder
4 chicken breast fillets, chopped
¼ cup cream
2 eggs

SPINACH FILLING
15g butter
1 clove garlic, crushed
1 bunch English spinach, chopped
¾ cup cooked rice
2 tablespoons cream
1 egg
¼ teaspoon ground nutmeg
TOMATO SAUCE
3 medium tomatoes, chopped
1 medium onion, chopped
1 tablespoon brown vinegar
½ teaspoon sugar

Boil, steam or microwave spinach until tender, drain well. Line base and side of greased 12cm x 23cm ovenproof

Hot Spinach Cheesecake.

HOT SPINACH CHEESECAKE

This recipe is unsuitable to freeze or microwave.

60g butter
1 cup finely crushed cheese biscuit crumbs
¼ cup grated parmesan cheese
SPINACH FILLING
2 bunches English spinach
3 bacon rashers, chopped
1 medium onion, chopped

250g packet cream cheese
125g feta cheese
300g carton sour cream
4 eggs, lightly beaten

Melt butter in saucepan, add biscuit crumbs, press evenly over base of greased 20cm springform tin, refrigerate 30 minutes.

Pour filling over biscuit base, stand on oven tray, bake in moderately slow oven for 1¼ hours or until golden brown and set. Sprinkle with cheese,

stand 10 minutes before cutting.

Spinach Filling: Boil, steam or microwave spinach until just tender, drain. Press excess liquid from spinach, chop spinach roughly.

Cook bacon and onion in frying pan, stirring constantly, until onion is soft. Beat cheeses in small bowl with electric mixer until smooth. Add sour cream and eggs, beat until combined. Transfer to large bowl, stir in spinach and bacon mixture.

113

STRAWBERRIES

Strawberries have been eaten for many centuries, but it was not until the Middle Ages that they were cultivated successfully.

STRAWBERRY RHUBARB SAUCE

Sauce can be made up to 3 days ahead or frozen for up to 2 months. Grand Marnier is an orange-flavoured liqueur. Serve sauce cold over ice-cream. Recipe unsuitable to microwave.

5 cups (425g) chopped rhubarb
500g strawberries
2 tablespoons water
1 cup castor sugar
1 tablespoon Grand Marnier
1 tablespoon finely chopped fresh
  mint

Combine rhubarb, strawberries, water and sugar in saucepan, stir constantly over heat, without boiling, until sugar is dissolved. Bring to boil, reduce heat, simmer, uncovered, 10 minutes or until thick; stir occasionally. Stir in liqueur and mint, blend or process until smooth. Cool, refrigerate before using.

Makes about 3½ cups.

STRAWBERRY SHORTCAKE

Shortcake can be cooked several days in advance or frozen for up to 2 months. Decorated shortcake can be made a day ahead. Grand Marnier is an orange-flavoured liqueur. Recipe unsuitable to microwave.

250g butter, softened
1 teaspoon grated lemon rind
3 teaspoons lemon juice

Strawberry Rhubarb Sauce.

China: Wedgwood

½ cup castor sugar
⅓ cup rice flour
1 cup self-raising flour
1⅓ cups plain flour
250g strawberries, halved
½ cup strawberry jam
1 tablespoon Grand Marnier

Beat butter, lemon rind, juice and sugar in small bowl with electric mixer until creamy (do not over-cream). Stir in sifted flours in 2 batches. Press ingredients together gently with floured hands, knead lightly until smooth. Press evenly into lightly greased 24cm recess flan tin. Bake in moderate oven for about 20 minutes or until lightly browned; cool in tin. Turn onto serving plate, decorate with strawberries.

Combine jam and liqueur in small saucepan, stir constantly over heat until combined, push through sieve to remove seeds. Cool slightly, brush evenly over strawberries. Serve with whipped cream.

▶

Strawberry Shortcake.

STRAWBERRIES

Bowls: Villeroy & Boch; table: Keyhole Furniture

*LEFT:
Strawberry
Cream Ice-
Cream.
BELOW:
Strawberry
Vinaigrette.*

▶ STRAWBERRY VINAIGRETTE

Recipe can be made up to 2 days
ahead, it is unsuitable to freeze.

250g strawberries
⅓ cup cider vinegar
1 cup olive oil
1 tablespoon canned green
 peppercorns, drained
½ teaspoon dried oregano leaves
1 teaspoon sugar
1 clove garlic, chopped
Blend or process all ingredients until
smooth. Store in jar in refrigerator. Use
as a salad dressing.
 Makes about 2½ cups.

STRAWBERRY CREAM ICE-CREAM

Ice-cream can be made up to 3 days
ahead; keep, covered, in freezer.

500g strawberries
2 x 300ml cartons thickened cream
1 cup icing sugar
Blend or process strawberries until
smooth. Beat cream and sifted icing
sugar together in large bowl with electric mixer until soft peaks form; fold in
strawberry purée. Pour mixture into
deep 23cm square cake pan, cover
with foil, freeze several hours or until
firm. Beat in large bowl or process mixture in several batches until smooth.
Return mixture to cake pan, cover,
freeze overnight until set.
 Makes about 2 litres.

Bowl: Wedgwood; jug and ladle: Reflections Gift Boutique

TAMARILLOS

The tamarillo (tree tomato) is native to South America and the Peruvian Andes; it is now grown in many tropical and sub-tropical countries. It is grown commercially in New Zealand. The skin is inedible. Peel with a sharp knife or cover with boiling water, drain immediately, then peel skin.

TAMARILLO APPLE TARTS WITH LEMON SAUCE

PASTRY
1½ cups plain flour
125g butter
2 egg yolks
1 tablespoon lemon juice, approximately

TAMARILLO APPLE FILLING
8 medium tamarillos, chopped
3 large apples, chopped
1 tablespoon lemon juice
⅔ cup sugar

TANGY LEMON SAUCE
1 cup sugar
2 tablespoons arrowroot
2 cups milk
3 egg yolks, lightly beaten
1 teaspoon grated lemon rind
⅓ cup lemon juice

►

China and cutlery: Kosta Boda

Tamarillo Apple Tarts with Lemon Sauce.

TAMARILLOS

▶ **Pastry:** Sift flour into bowl, rub in butter. Add egg yolks and enough lemon juice to make ingredients cling together. Press dough into ball, cover, refrigerate 30 minutes.

Divide pastry into 6, roll each piece large enough to line 6 x 11cm flan tins; trim edges. Cover pastry with grease-proof paper, fill with dried beans or rice. Bake in moderately hot oven 5 minutes, remove paper and beans, bake 5 minutes or until golden brown.

Divide filling into pastry cases, decorate with remaining pastry. Bake in moderate oven 20 minutes; serve hot or cold with warm sauce.

Tamarillo Apple Filling: Combine tamarillos, apples and lemon juice in saucepan, bring to boil, reduce heat, simmer 10 minutes; stir occasionally. Add sugar, stir until dissolved, without boiling; bring to boil, reduce heat, simmer 15 minutes; stir occasionally. Cool to room temperature.

Tangy Lemon Sauce: Combine sugar and arrowroot in saucepan, gradually stir in milk, stir constantly over heat until mixture boils and thickens; remove from heat. Quickly stir in egg yolks, then lemon rind and juice.

Makes 6.

TAMARILLO CUSTARD SLICES

This recipe is unsuitable to freeze or microwave.

½ x 375g packet puff pastry
3 medium tamarillos, sliced
½ cup strawberry jam
RICH CUSTARD FILLING
2 egg yolks
¼ cup castor sugar
¼ cup milk
1 tablespoon plain flour
1 tablespoon cornflour
1 teaspoon vanilla essence
1 tablespoon castor sugar, extra
½ cup milk, extra
125g unsalted butter

Cut pastry in half, roll each piece into a 20cm x 25cm rectangle, place on greased trays, bake in hot oven for about 10 minutes or until lightly browned; cool.

Place pastry shapes onto serving plates, spread each with a thin layer of custard. Place remaining custard into a piping bag fitted with a plain tube, pipe custard around edges of pastry shapes; fill centres with tamarillos; refrigerate until firm.

Warm jam in saucepan, push through sieve to remove seeds, brush slices gently all over with jam. Refrigerate 1 hour before serving.

Rich Custard Filling: Blend or process egg yolks, sugar, milk, flour, cornflour and essence until smooth. Combine extra sugar and extra milk in saucepan, bring to boil, gradually add to egg mixture while motor is operating. Return mixture to saucepan, stir constantly over heat until mixture boils and thickens; cover, cool to room temperature.

Beat butter in small bowl with electric mixer until as white as possible, gradually beat in cold custard.

Tamarillo Custard Slices

China: Wedgwood/Coalport; knife: Whitehill Silverplate Co.

ROAST DUCKLING WITH TAMARILLO SAUCE

This recipe is unsuitable to freeze or microwave.

**Size 15 duckling
1 tablespoon olive oil
freshly ground black pepper
2 tablespoons brown sugar
2 tablespoons water
8 medium tamarillos, chopped
6 green shallots, chopped
1 teaspoon French mustard**

Secure openings of duckling with skewers. Place duckling in baking dish, brush with oil, season with pepper. Bake in moderate oven for about 1¼ hours or until tender; brush duckling occasionally with pan juices.

Combine sugar, water and tamarillos in saucepan, bring to boil; reduce heat, simmer, covered, 5 minutes. Remove from heat, push through sieve; discard seeds.

Remove duckling from dish, keep warm, reserve ¼ cup strained pan juices. Combine pan juices, shallots and mustard in saucepan, cook 2 minutes, stirring. Add tamarillo purée, stir until heated through; serve with sliced duckling .

Serves 4.

China: Wedgwood; cutlery: Whitehill Silverplate Co.

Roast Duckling with Tamarillo Sauce.

TOMATOES

Tomatoes originated in the Andes area and were introduced throughout Europe and the western world around the 17th century. Tomatoes are now cultivated in many sizes, shapes, and colours. To peel: cut a small cross through the skin at the bottom of the fruit (not stem end), cover with boiling water, stand a minute, then place into cold water; peel skin.

Tomato Apricot Chutney.

TOMATOES

► TOMATO APRICOT CHUTNEY

Store chutney in refrigerator for up to a year. This recipe is unsuitable to freeze or microwave.

250g dried apricots
2 cups water
2 teaspoons oil
2 teaspoons yellow mustard seeds
2 teaspoons cumin seeds
8 large tomatoes, peeled, chopped
4 medium onions, finely chopped
1 cup orange juice
⅓ cup lemon juice
⅓ cup tomato paste
2 cups white vinegar
2 cups sugar
1 tablespoon light soya sauce
1 tablespoon grated fresh ginger

Combine apricots and water in saucepan, bring to boil, boil 5 minutes.

Heat oil in frying pan, add mustard and cumin seeds, cook, stirring, for about 4 minutes or until lightly browned; cool. Crush seeds with rolling pin. Combine seeds with undrained apricot mixture and tomatoes in large heavy-based pan. Add onions, juices, tomato paste, vinegar, sugar, soya sauce and ginger. Stir constantly over heat, without boiling, until sugar is dissolved, bring to boil, reduce heat, simmer 1 hour, uncovered or until mixture is as thick as desired. Pour into hot sterilised jars, seal when cold.

Makes about 5 cups.

SPICY TOMATO SAUCE

Sauce can be made up to 3 days ahead or frozen for up to 6 months.

8 large tomatoes, chopped
2 large onions, chopped
2 cloves garlic, crushed
½ cup dry red wine
½ teaspoon chilli powder
¼ cup brown sugar
1 tablespoon French mustard

Combine all ingredients in saucepan, bring to boil, reduce heat, simmer, uncovered, 30 minutes (or microwave on HIGH for about 30 minutes) or until mixture is reduced by about one-third. Blend or process until smooth, sieve, discard skin and seeds.

Makes about 3 cups.

PASTA WITH TOMATOES, OLIVES AND ARTICHOKES

Serve sauce hot, warm or cold over cooked pasta. This recipe is unsuitable to freeze or microwave.

4 large tomatoes, peeled, chopped
1 cup (185g) black olives, chopped
400g can artichokes, drained, quartered

Spicy Tomato Sauce.

Jar: Accoutrement; wire basket: The Country Trader.

75g can anchovy fillets, drained, chopped
375g pasta
FRESH HERB DRESSING
¼ cup olive oil
¼ cup lemon juice
¼ cup chopped fresh basil
2 tablespoons chopped fresh parsley

Combine tomatoes, olives, artichokes and anchovies in bowl. Add pasta gradually to large saucepan of boiling water. Boil rapidly, uncovered, for about 10 minutes or until just tender, drain. Combine pasta with tomato mixture, add dressing before serving.

Fresh Herb Dressing: Combine all ingredients in jar; shake well.

Serves 6.

Pasta with Tomatoes, Olives and Artichokes.

Serving ware: Villa Italiana; tiles: Pazotti

ZUCCHINI

Zucchini is the Italian name for small marrows; the French name is courgette. Zucchini belong to the vegetable marrow family or summer squash family. This species originated in Mexico and Central America.

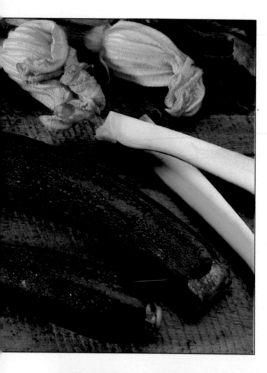

MUSHROOM PRAWN ZUCCHINI

This recipe is unsuitable to freeze or microwave.

5 medium zucchini
½ cup stale breadcrumbs
½ cup grated tasty cheese
175g cooked prawns, shelled, finely chopped
30g mushrooms, finely chopped
1 tablespoon chopped fresh parsley
30g butter, melted

Boil, steam or microwave zucchini until just tender, drain. Cut zucchini in half lengthwise, scoop pulp from centres with teaspoon. Combine zucchini pulp, breadcrumbs, cheese, prawns, mushrooms, parsley and butter in bowl, mix well. Spoon mixture into shells, grill until lightly browned.

Makes 10.

RATATOUILLE CREPES

Unfilled crêpes can be frozen for up to 2 months. Recipe unsuitable to freeze or microwave.

425g can tomatoes
1 tablespoon oil
1 small onion, sliced
1 clove garlic, crushed
4 medium zucchini, chopped
1 medium green pepper, chopped
2 teaspoons tomato paste
¼ teaspoon dried oregano leaves
2 tablespoons grated tasty cheese
CREPES
½ cup plain flour
2 eggs
1 tablespoon oil
¾ cup milk
HERB AND WINE SAUCE
2 teaspoons oil
1 clove garlic, crushed
1 tablespoon dry white wine
1 tablespoon chopped fresh parsley

Drain tomatoes, reserve ¼ cup liquid for sauce. Heat oil in large frying pan, add onion and garlic, cook, stirring,

Mushroom Prawn Zucchini.

Napkin: The Design Store; wooden basket: Country House

Ratatouille Crêpes.

Zucchini Potato Soup.

Bowls : The Bay Tree

▶ until onion is soft. Add zucchini, pepper, tomatoes, paste and oregano, cook over low heat for about 20 minutes or until vegetables are tender; cool. Place tablespoonfuls of mixture onto crêpes, fold in quarters.

Place crêpes in single layer in greased ovenproof dish, cover, bake in moderate oven for about 10 minutes or until heated through. Serve with sauce, sprinkle with cheese.

Crêpes: Sift flour into bowl, make well in centre, add eggs, oil and 2 tablespoons of the milk; beat until smooth. Beat in remaining milk; refrigerate 30 minutes. Heat heavy-based pan, grease with butter. Pour a thin layer of batter into pan, brown on one side, turn, brown other side; turn onto plate. Repeat with remaining batter.

Herb and Wine Sauce: Heat oil in small saucepan, add garlic, cook, stirring, for

1 minute. Add reserved tomato liquid and wine. Bring to boil, reduce heat, simmer, uncovered, 3 minutes; stir in parsley just before serving.

ZUCCHINI POTATO SOUP

Soup can be prepared up to a day ahead. Recipe unsuitable to freeze.

30g butter
1 medium onion, chopped
1 teaspoon dry mustard
3 medium zucchini, chopped
2 medium potatoes, chopped
2 small chicken stock cubes, crumbled
2 cups water
2 tablespoons grated parmesan cheese
½ cup sour cream
3 medium zucchini, extra
30g butter, extra

Melt butter in large saucepan, add onion and mustard, cook, stirring, until onion is soft (or microwave on HIGH for about 3 minutes). Add zucchini and potatoes, cook 5 minutes (or microwave on HIGH for about 3 minutes); stir occasionally.

Add stock cubes and water, bring to boil, reduce heat, simmer 15 minutes or until vegetables are tender (or microwave on HIGH for about 7 minutes). Blend or process soup until smooth. Stir in cheese and sour cream, return to pan.

Cut extra zucchini into fine strips. Melt extra butter in frying pan, add zucchini, cook, stirring, for about 2 minutes or until just tender (or microwave on HIGH for about 1 minute). Add zucchini mixture to soup, reheat without boiling.

Serves 4.

GLOSSARY

ALMONDS: use commercially ground almonds when recipe specifies.

ARROWROOT: a thickening ingredient; cornflour can be substituted.

BACON: rashers are bacon slices.

BEETROOT: regular round beet.

BICARBONATE OF SODA: baking soda, a component of baking powder.

BREADCRUMBS, Stale: use 1 or 2 day old white or wholemeal bread made into crumbs by grating, blending or processing. Packaged: use commercially packaged breadcrumbs.

BUTTER: we used salted (sweet) butter unless otherwise specified; a good quality cooking margarine can be used if preferred.
1 stick butter = 125g butter.

CHEESE, Tasty: use a firm good-tasting cheddar cheese.

CHICKEN: numbers indicate the weight, for example: No. 13 chicken weighs 1.3kg. Breast fillets: skinless and boneless. Breast on the bone: sold either whole or as half breasts, usually with skin. Drumsticks: leg with skin intact. Marylands: joined leg and thigh with skin intact. Thigh fillets: skinless and boneless.

CHILLIES, Fresh: are available in many different types and sizes. The small ones (bird's eye or bird peppers) are the hottest. Use tight-fitting gloves when handling and chopping fresh chillies as they can burn your skin. The seeds are the hottest part of the chillies, so remove them if you want to reduce the heat content of recipes. Powder: the Asian variety of the powder is the hottest and is made from dried chillies; it can be used as a substitute for fresh chillies in the proportion of ½ teaspoon ground chilli powder to 1 medium chopped chilli. Sauce: we used a hot

Chinese variety. It consists of chillies, salt and vinegar. We used it sparingly so that you can easily increase the amounts in recipes to suit your taste.

COOKING SALT: a coarse salt (not the same as fine table salt).

CORNMEAL: it is also known as polenta.

CORN SYRUP: an imported product available in supermarkets, delicatessens and health food stores. It is available in light or dark — either one can be substituted for the other.

CREAM: we have specified thickened (whipping) cream when necessary in recipes; cream is simply a light pouring cream, also known as half 'n' half. Sour: a thick commercially cultured soured cream. Light sour: a less dense commercially cultured soured cream.

CUSTARD POWDER: pudding mix.

ESSENCE: extract.

FIVE SPICE POWDER: a mixture of ground spices which includes cinnamon, cloves, fennel, star anise and Szechwan pepper.

FLOUR: Plain: all-purpose flour. Self-raising: substitute plain (all purpose) flour and baking powder in the proportion of ¾ metric cup plain flour to 2 level metric teaspoons baking powder, sift together several times before using. If using an 8oz measuring cup, use 1 cup plain flour to 2 level metric teaspoons baking powder. Cornflour: cornstarch. Rice flour: ground rice. Wholemeal plain: wholewheat all-purpose flour. Wholemeal self-raising: use wholewheat all-purpose flour and baking powder in the proportions given in plain flour instructions.

GINGER, Fresh ginger: ginger root. Glacé ginger: crystallised ginger can be substituted; rinse off the sugar with warm water, dry ginger well before using.

GRILL, GRILLER: broil, broiler.

HERBS, Fresh: we have specified when to use fresh or dried herbs, or given alternative measurements when possible. We used dried (not ground) herbs in the proportion of 1:4 for fresh herbs, e.g., 1 teaspoon dried herbs instead of

▶

APPROXIMATE CUP AND SPOON CONVERSION CHART

Australian	American & British
1 cup	1¼ cups
¾ cup	1 cup
⅔ cup	¾ cup
½ cup	⅔ cup
⅓ cup	½ cup
¼ cup	⅓ cup
2 tablespoons	¼ cup
1 tablespoon	3 teaspoons

CUP AND SPOON MEASURES

Recipes in this book use this standard metric equipment approved by the Australian Standards Association:
(a) 250 millilitre cup for measuring liquids. A litre jug (capacity 4 cups) is also available.
(b) a graduated set of four cups — measuring 1 cup, half, third and quarter cup — for items such as flour, sugar, etc. When measuring in these fractional cups, level off at the brim.
(c) a graduated set of four spoons: tablespoon (20 millilitre liquid capacity), teaspoon (5 millilitre), half and quarter teaspoons. The Australian, British and American teaspoon each has 5 ml capacity.

All spoon measurements are level.
Note: We have used large eggs with an average weight of 61g each in all recipes.

OVEN TEMPERATURES

Electric Temperatures	Celsius	Fahrenheit	Gas Temperatures	Celsius	Fahrenheit
Very slow	120	250	Very slow	120	250
Slow	150	300	Slow	150	300
Moderately slow	160-180	325-350	Moderately slow	160	325
Moderate	180-200	375-400	Moderate	180	350
Moderately hot	210-230	425-450	Moderately hot	190	375
Hot	240-250	475-500	Hot	200	400
Very hot	260	525-550	Very hot	230	450

GLOSSARY

4 teaspoons (1 tablespoon) chopped fresh herbs. **Ground:** use powdered form. **Dried:** use dehydrated leaf of herb. When fresh herbs are specified but unavailable use ¼ of the dried leaf variety instead of the fresh; e.g., use 1 teaspoon dried basil leaves as a substitute for 1 tablespoon (4 teaspoons) chopped fresh basil. This is not recommended when more than a tablespoon of fresh herbs is to be substituted.

HOISIN SAUCE: a thick sweet Chinese barbecue sauce made from salted black beans, onions and garlic.

HONEY SNAP PEAS: also known as sugar peas. Snow peas can be substituted.

KUMARA: a variety of sweet potato; it is orange in colour.

LAMINGTON PAN: a rectangular slab pan with a depth of about 4cm.

LEMON BUTTER: lemon curd or lemon cheese.

LETTUCE: we used mostly iceberg, radicchio, mignonette and butter lettuce; any variety of lettuce can be used.

MARSALA: a sweet fortified wine, traditionally from Italy.

MUESLI: granola.

MUSTARD, SEEDED: a French style of textured mustard with crushed mustard seeds.

OIL: we used a light polyunsaturated salad oil unless otherwise specified.

OYSTER SAUCE: a rich, brown bottled sauce made from oysters, cooked in salt and soya sauce.

PIMIENTOS: sweet red peppers preserved in brine in cans or jars.

PORK, Butterfly: skinless, boneless mid-loin chop which has been split in half and opened out flat. **Fillets:** skinless, boneless eye-fillet from the loin. **Steaks:** schnitzels, usually cut from the leg or rump.

RIND: zest.

SHALLOTS, Golden: members of the onion family, with a delicate onion/garlic flavour. **Green shallots:** known as spring onions in some Australian States, also called scallions in some other countries.

SOYA SAUCE: made from fermented soya beans; we used 2 types, the light and dark variety. The light sauce is generally used with white meat and the darker variety with red meat dishes.

SPRING ONIONS: vegetables with small white bulbs and long green leaves.

STOCK CUBE: a small stock cube is equivalent to 1 teaspoon powdered bouillon (stock powder).

SUGAR: we used a coarse granulated table sugar unless otherwise stated. **Castor:** fine granulated table sugar. **Brown:** soft brown sugar. **Icing:** confectioners', or powdered sugar. We used the icing sugar mixture, not pure icing sugar. **Raw:** natural, light granulated sugar.

SULTANAS: seedless white raisins.

SWEET BISCUIT CRUMBS: any plain sweet biscuit (or cookie) can be used.

TAMARIND SAUCE: is made from the acid tasting fruit of the tamarind tree. If unavailable, soak about 30g dried tamarind in a cup of water, stand 10 minutes. Squeeze the pulp as dry as possible and use the flavoured water.

TERIYAKI SAUCE: a sauce based on the lighter Japanese soya sauce; it contains sugar, spices and vinegar.

TOMATO PUREE: known as tomato sauce in some other countries. You can use canned tomato purée or a purée of fresh, ripe tomatoes made by blending or processing the required amount for the recipe. **Sauce:** tomato ketchup.

VEAL: Cutlets: cut from the rib and loin. **Steaks:** schnitzels, cut from the leg. **Chops:** cut from the rib and loin.

WHITE FISH: simply means non-oily fish, and could include bream, flathead, whiting, snapper, jewfish and ling.

WHOLEMEAL: wholewheat.

INDEX

INDEX